ALTIPLANO

JAMIE GRANT

To Mike,
All best wishes and
hope to catch up soon,

Jamie

First published in Great Britain in 2019
by Wolf Dog Press

Copyright © Jamie Grant

A copy of this books is available from the British Library

ISBN: 978 1 913218 52 2

Typesetting and cover design by
Raspberry Creative Type, Edinburgh

Cover photography by Jamie Grant

Printed and bound in Great Britain by www.biddles.co.uk

Wolfdog Press
Lyon Lodge
Glen Lyon
Perthshire
Scotland
PH15 2PP

www.wolfdogpress.co.uk

To Fiona

From this hour I ordain myself loos'd of limits
and imaginary lines
Going where I list my own master total and absolute
Listening to others considering well what they say
Pausing, searching, receiving, contemplating
Gently, but with undeniable will,
divesting myself of all the holds that would hold me
I inhale great draughts of space,
the East and the West are mine
and the North and South are mine.
I am larger, better than I thought,
I didn't know I held such goodness

From the Song of the Open Road (1856)
Walt Whitman

CONTENTS

INTRODUCTION

It was my father Nigel's love of the high Andes that first brought me to Bolivia. As a geologist he was sent on lengthy field trips to the Bolivian highlands in the mid-seventies, carrying out surveys of copper deposits in the mountains near Oruro. His PhD from Imperial College London based on his findings – completely unreadable to my unscientific mind – sits in one of my desk drawers together with several of his rock samples.

I occasionally roll these cylinders of rock over in my hands. I have always loved the way they feel; smooth, cool and impervious to change. They have marbled patterns of mottled green, laced through with flashes of cobalt blue. My father would decipher these patterns, stitching together vast stretches of geological time with a handful of measured sentences. To me the true meaning of these rocks is deeper, hidden in the silent poetry of the Earth.

I vividly remember Dad coming home to Scotland after one of his many lengthy trips to the Bolivian Andes. He appeared at the door and lifted my little brother, Charlie, and me up into his arms, spinning us around in the cramped hall of our cottage in the West Highlands. His clothes smelt of smoke, animal oil and dung. That

1

night he sat by the fire in a long red poncho and a hat with ear flaps, listening to vinyl records of Andean panpipes and let us touch the long moustache that he had grown on his travels. I think that my American mother, Lucy, was as bewildered as we were by his faintly bizarre homecomings.

Over the years my father told stories from the Bolivian Altiplano that stoked my imagination. He talked about the women in the witches' market in La Paz who sell charms for secret magic ceremonies. Of mountains streaked with all the colours of the rainbow by their rich mineral deposits. The great lake high in the Andes where people travel on boats built of reeds. He often mentioned the light, how sharp it is, how you have to wear sunglasses in the snow to prevent going blind.

I used to sit on the old pier at Arnisdale, staring across the Atlantic straits to southern Skye beyond. I imagined that this other country of limitless horizons lay just beyond those hills. In my mind's eye it was wild, open and far more exciting than home (by the time I was twelve years old I had introduced bare breasted Amazonian women to the picture). It would have to be, after all, a pretty fantastic place to tempt my father away from us so often.

When I finally made it to Bolivia for the first time in the mid 1990s it felt like a distant homecoming. I'll never forget arriving in La Paz at night on that first journey across the Atacama desert and into the Andes in a single carriage diesel train from Arica. The train laboured up the *cordillera* at only a few miles an hour until we reached the high plain. From there the narrow-gauge tracks glistened far ahead of us in the burning sand like two slender, silver backed snakes. The Bolivian border back then was a wooden shack, not much larger than a Glastonbury portaloo. Two guards emerged out of it to nonchalantly wave us on with brown beer bottles.

We arrived at the outskirts of La Paz at the centre of an immaculate night. Teetering on the highest edge of a deep canyon, the near vertical sides of the city looked like a deep sea of stars. With the constellations overhead, so clear at 4,000 metres, it felt like we were abandoning the earth altogether to beetle through outer space.

'Here in Bolivia life is very slow and peaceful,' the taxi driver blithely told us as we raced down town to our hostel. I caught sight of a starlit skyline of ragged peaks before being plunged into a gridlock of traffic around Plaza San Francisco.

The city spilled around us in chaotic disorder. A thunderstorm was breaking and shop keepers, traffic police and Saturday night revellers were scuttling for shelter from a torrent of rain. The streets ran with water, rubbish and stray dogs. It all slipped past my window like the nocturnal imaginings of a fitful dream. I felt I had parachuted from the twenty-first century into a medieval citadel or a vast army encampment on the eve of some ancient battle.

The first thing I recognised when I stepped out of my hostel the next morning was my father's description of the light. A fierce, white sunshine that cut every detail of the city into razor sharp relief. Beyond, the mountains looked beaten flat like giant billboards in its glare. I wondered if they would suddenly collapse in a strong wind, leaving nothing more than a tangle of scaffolding and dust.

I was so captivated by this first visit to Bolivia that I studied an MA on Latin America in London, before returning to La Paz to work as a journalist for three years. During this time I camped with indigenous tribes in the Bolivian Amazon, ate sheep brains with an Aymara family in a remote highland village, caught Hepatitis A and Typhus (at the same time), fell in love, almost drowned while rafting the Coroico river and narrowly avoided being deported by the then president Hugo Banzer for reporting on human rights abuses. When I decided to settle back in Scotland a Bolivian friend told me 'You will always carry a small piece of the Andes in your heart.' He didn't warn me that this part of myself would divide my soul and eventually draw me back.

A singular event propelled be back to Bolivia. My father died suddenly in Chile, where he was living with his Brazilian second wife and their daughter Claudia. He fell off his bike on a Sunday ride near their home in Santiago. The neighbour who found him unconscious but still alive phoned both the hospital and the community priest. It was the priest who reached him first and my father died in his arms before the ambulance even arrived.

I flew to Santiago the next day, my sense of shock amplified by the sudden journey out of a dreich Highland winter into a blazing South American summer. The small church in Las Condes was overflowing with mourners I didn't know. I stood at the entrance next to my brother afterwards to be hugged and kissed by a procession of teary-eyed strangers.

Stepping into the vestibule to look at my father one last time behind the oval window of a sleek black coffin was the hardest thing I have ever done. Only once there I felt an odd sense of relief. The profile in the coffin was Nigel, but the father that I had come to say goodbye to had clearly already left. I stood there for what seemed like an eternity with no idea where he had gone, or how I could find my way back to the man that I so loved but felt like I barely knew.

At the wake that evening I slipped into Dad's study to escape the crush of mourners. Opening the top drawer of a desk I found his field watch. It was a reassuringly heavy chunk of 1970s technology with a big black face and the words *'navigator timer, water 70m proof'* written in tiny script in the centre.

The watch's frozen hands recorded the slender moment of 3:22pm and 43 seconds, the exact point that this time-piece's mechanised momentum unwound to a full stop. I wondered if there is some clockwork buried inside us all that ticks down to our prescribed departure. Or if the universe is just a game of chance – numbers picked from a rolling ball at the back of a dimly lit bingo hall.

Dad once told me this watch was the one constant on all his field trips because it was so indestructible. It didn't even need a battery, winding itself back up with the boundless swing of his arm. Maybe he loved it because it felt like certainty on his wrist, a solid artefact of interlocking precision to help his scientific mind sub-divide and interpret the world.

I stood for a long time feeling the watch's solidness in my hand. If grief has a weight then this was it. Numbed to the buzz of conversation in the hall outside I studied the tiny watch window's lattice of scratches across the glass. Each fine line marked for me a momentary intersection in his life. I wondered if I could interpret them, like the creases on a palm or an encrypted map that I could follow, or maybe even link up.

To me all these faint contours led back to one distant region, the Altiplano. That heartland that had shaped both mine and my father's lives. Here I could be a different kind of explorer, seeking out memories rather than mineral samples. I so desperately wanted to piece together the threadbare fragments of my family tapestry, to somehow re-imagine our lives back into a single, coherent image.

LA PAZ

The plane was cold, dimly lit and smelt musty. The blue, tatty décor must have been around 20 years out of date and the two hostesses were reassuringly rude. In-flight entertainment was left to the flight attendant. 'Welcome aboard,' boomed a Texan accent on the intercom as we buckled ourselves in. In the dim light at the other end of the plane I could just about make out a shiny pate, beaming smile and stars and stripes tie.

It had been obvious from the moment we stepped on to the American Airlines plane in Miami that we were headed for a destination less travelled. Gone was the high tech entertainment on the transatlantic flight from London, with 40 films available at the touch of a button on the back of each headrest. Gone were the manicured air hostesses with their courtesy smiles. Gone too was the in-flight magazine promoting 'The Chivas Life,' the world packaged up unto a series of luxury entertainments.

'Would those of you who have never been to Bolivia please put your hands up?' our attendant asked. On a show of hands he waved and said it was great to see some newcomers to his 'second most favourite country.' 'I am confident that you all are going to have a great time in Bolivia, even in the rarefied air,' he drawled. 'The politics might be a little tight but the people are just fantastic.'

Exhausted from the previous flight over the Atlantic and dazed by Miami airport's bewildering nexus of transmigrating souls I closed my eyes and tried to gather my thoughts. It felt as though I was on the final leg of a journey started by my father. He took a similar flight to La Paz in 1976 to start field research in the Andes for his PhD.

Dad's research trip to Bolivia can't have seemed very different at the time to all his other flights to exotic corners of the world. He spent much of his life jetting around the globe in pursuit of rocks, mineral deposits and sediment formations. But he was a pioneer to me that night in 1976, unwittingly opening up a connection to a region that ran on far beyond his own lifetime. How could he have imagined that his son would follow a similar trajectory? That decades apart we would both be hurtling through the night towards the same uncertain destination.

I wondered if he was gripped by the same sense of awe as we finally climbed under a full moon into the Andes. The mountain's jagged ridges powered up out of the plains like gatekeepers to a high blown, forgotten land. 'They must be sleeping,' I thought to myself as we teetered unchallenged between two frozen peaks, their moonlit crests flowing with white manes. Beyond the mountains lay the Bolivian Altiplano, a high plateau of scorched sunlight and ochre earth that stretches some 800 km through the central Andes and is bound by two great mountain chains, the *Cordillera Real* in the West and *Cordillera Occidental* in the East.

Thrown up into the thin air by the collision of the Nazca and South American tectonic plates some 40 million years ago, the Altiplano covers a bigger surface area than Britain, most of it around 4,000 metres above sea level. To get your head around these heights you have to try and picture four Ben Nevises sitting on top of each other. This expanse of high plains has glowered in my imagination like Jack's castle in the clouds ever since I first visited Bolivia. Together with the Himalayas, the Altiplano really is the roof of the world.

For me the final approach by plane into El Alto International Airport has always felt like a Mars landing. Dawn was breaking as the plane descended, the sun streaking a pencil line of egg yoke yellow along the earth's delicately arched horizon. The fire then flamed across the night's deep blue, lifting the veil of darkness to reveal a landscape beyond measure. There didn't appear to be any Tierra Firma to touch down on at all. It felt more like we were falling into an infinite ellipse of shimmering dust and light.

The plane banked sharply and La Paz's sprawling twin city of El Alto swung into view. Fanning out from the area known as the Ceja (the eyebrow), El Alto was thrown up by mainly indigenous Aymara migrants from the mines and the countryside in a few decades. A rebel city, born out of poverty, drought and neo-liberal reform, El Alto was only officially recognised in 1988 and has since gained a well-earned reputation for political ferment, lawlessness and outright rebellion. With a population of over 2.3 million the city now sprawls over 350 square kilometres around the world's highest commercial airport. And yet from the air there is an odd tranquillity to the city's tumbledown disorder as we descended in the dawn's gilded light towards the runway.

There is no such thing as a soft landing at El Alto Airport. At 4,000 metres above sea level the 'rarefied' air gives less resistance to a large lump of metal hurtling through space. The main runway is 4km long to make up for the thin air and aircraft have to be modified with special tyres to handle the high take off and landing speeds.

We skipped along the runway like a stone skimmed across a loch. By the time the blur of tarmac came into focus I had convinced myself that we are going to overshoot it completely. I wasn't alone. My fellow passengers burst into spontaneous applause as we slowed to a halt. It was only the seatbelt sign that stopped the pilot from receiving a standing ovation.

Walking off the plane the altitude slowed everyone's pace around me. Time felt stretched and my limbs were suddenly heavy and sluggish. It was the strangest of sensations, as though we had been beamed to another planet where the air is a different mix, thin and insubstantial. Oxygen is such a luxury in this town that it is sold to befuddled travellers to gasp on. The first kiosk at the baggage pick-up stocks a prominent display of 'Oxyshot' aerosol canisters and the smarter hotels in town offer whole bottles of compressed 'O' for the weary traveller to hook up to at night.

From the airport you don't so much arrive in La Paz as spin like a pinball into what is locally known as *El Hueco* (the Hole). Travelling down the main highway that links the two cities, my taxi tipped over the canyon's edge and traversed steeply down towards the centre of La Paz. In the years since I worked here I had often dreamt of this spellbinding moment of return.

The Choqueyapu valley opened out below us, a wide bowl of light framed by the Andes ragged crown. Founded La Cuidad de Nuestra Señora de la Paz (City of our Lady of Peace) in 1548 by the Spanish captain Alonso de Mendoza, the valley was chosen for its fresh water and ample woodland. Mendoza lay the founding stone in the indigenous village of Laja next to the clear running waters of the Choqueyapu, named by the locals as 'the golden river.'

Today the river Choqueyapu is so polluted with effluence and industrial waste that large sections of it have simply been entombed in concrete and it is mainly streets and houses rather than trees that now cling to the valley slopes in a precipitous tangle of adobe, brick and wire. From every angle windows reflect and amplify the intense Incan sun. The city centre, much of it an odd collection of 1970s apartment buildings far below, is completely dwarfed by the drama of its surroundings.

It isn't the city itself but the mountain above it that defines La Paz. The 6,400 metre peak of Illimani dominates the skyline. I remember being transfixed by my first clear view of its snow-laden slopes, lit on fire by the setting sun while La Paz slumbered in shadow below. Its glaciers have since receded with the onset of climate change, no doubt contributing to the severe water shortages that La Paz and El Alto have suffered in recent years.

I have always preferred Illimani partially obscured by cloud, its constant presence still casting a shrouded eye over the city. Regarded as a protective spirit, the mountain is rarely uncloaked from its wreath of mist during the rainy season. As the Bolivian poet Jaime Saenz writes:

"Although Illimani is there, it is something that you can't see

What you see is the sky, the space of the
mountain, not the mountain
The sky of the mountain gathers dusk in the
afternoon, at night the Southern Cross
It isn't the mountain that one sees. It is the
presence of the mountain

As we descended by taxi into the heart of the city I realised just how much Illimani mirrored my father's place in my life. His physical form may have lifted into the mist but his presence still loomed over me like a vast, ambivalent shadow. He has hung over me like this, a cloud that wouldn't shift, ever since my parent's marriage fell apart when I was nine years old.

Luckily my parents were very discreet, sparing my little brother Charlie and me the hurt and despair of a messy divorce. We were living in Amsterdam in Holland at the time and the only picture I have in my head of this moment is blue trunks being packed up in a living room wallpapered with big 1970s orange and chocolate brown swirls. In my mind's eye I picture my mother frenetically busy, sweeping Charlie and me along on a mini tsunami wave of love and bullish determination. Only much later did I understand how heartbroken she must have been. That Nigel was and remained the one true love of her life.

Mum, Charlie and I went on to live like refugees for a year with my American grandmother in a low wooden house in the New England woods outside of Boston. Dad was transferred by the minerals company he worked for to Rio de Janeiro. From America we initially went back to our little cottage in Glenelg. After a year we moved down to Devon where Mum valiantly sailed us through our teenage years alone. Dad went on to re-marry and spend the rest of his life in South America.

Charlie and I struggled to make sense of this long fragmentation. Our father, already so often away on field trips, had now completely vanished from our lives. It was as though he had decided one day to float out the window to Neverland, leaving us only his shadow.

Dad once told me that on his first visit to Bolivia in 1976 he stayed in one of the many hostels that crowd around the Witches' Market in La Paz. This was one of the few certainties I had of his movements on this trip so many years ago. So I booked into a hostel in the thick of the old town as well, an old colonial building designed around two elegant courtyards on Calle Sagarnaga.

My second floor room had high ceilings and a green, wooden patio door that opened onto a narrow terrace. I squeezed gingerly onto it, unseen in a city that had no hold on me. From here I looked straight onto the imposing outline of the cathedral of San Francisco – founded in 1548, the formidable stone and terracotta walls threw half of the cobbled street below into deep shadow.

Sagarnaga remains a frenetic meeting point between two disparate peoples: the indigenous Aymara and the 21st century backpacker. Every doorway is overhung with gaudy advertisements for tours around the country or with racks of handmade textiles and factory produced imitations. The Aymara traders sit surrounded by their blankets, silver antiques and sugary drinks, while an endless parade of altitude weary tourists stream by in a succession of colourful hats.

Walk down Sagarnaga and you never know what is going to be offered to you: a stuffed armadillo, an amulet to drive away evil spirits, an umbrella to ward off the rain. Traders pushing wooden carts laden with clothes, electrical goods and toasted nuts were overtaken by businessmen in ill-fitting suits and greased back hair. Several determined looking mountaineers loaded their packs and climbing equipment onto the back of a minibus. An Aymara woman darted back and forth dispensing glasses of bright red jelly topped with whipped cream.

Shoe shiners, mostly young boys, sat on their little wooden boxes in balaclavas pointing out the dusty shoes of passers by. All the while minibuses lurched down Sagarnaga's steep incline, each with a kid shouting out route stops in a furious rap: El Prado, Seis de Augusto, Cota Cota, Orbrajes, Chasquipampa. It was as though they were calling the city's chaotic streets to order.

I noticed one street seller sitting alongside a row of small mirrors propped up on the wall. They tipped up to the sky in the dusking alley and caught a sharp reflection of the brilliant sky. From my elevated spot they didn't look like mirrors at all. It appeared to me as though this trader was a purveyor of oblong parcels of pure Andean light.

And at the back of it all was the smell, an indescribable scent that could only be La Paz. It wasn't really singular, more a shifting medley of different notes as bitter sweet as the city that embodies them. Dominant was the odour of diesel fumes from El Prado. Huge belching black clouds of the stuff billowed out of the ancient buses that creaked up the central drag with drivers as old and leathery as their interiors. But I caught other notes, like the slow roasting chicken '*al spiedo*,' browning on rotating spits. Or could it be *salchipapa*, the impossibly red, sliced sausage of dubious provenance (rumoured to be street dog) with fries.

There was a sweet baking smell that must be the pastry that makes up the delicious *saltenas* and *empanadas*, sold on every street corner. There was also a rich, fragrant lift of incense – someone somewhere was burning the wood *palo santo,* maybe for a magic ritual. And cutting through it all was a sharp tang of ammonia from the city's dodgy drains. Used to Scotland where everything smells damp, here the city is dry and hard, almost acrid, until the rains come in thunderous bouts from November to temporarily wash the streets clean of their sins again.

And through it all I pictured my dad walking, always walking. In my mind's eye he was dressed in his trademark brown flared cords and a blue Guernsey. Although a young man on his first visit to La Paz he still took it easy, a combination of the altitude and his own deliberate stride. I imagined him stopping to gently haggle with a street trader for a poncho or woven blanket. He especially liked the black textiles with red mythical creatures from the town of Tarabuco, south-east of Sucre.

If he had wandered on up the steep street he would have been quickly lost in the sprawling Buenos Aires' market, a maze of narrow alleyways selling mainly cut-price clothes, electrical gadgets and furniture. Keep going and he would have reached a long, tented area dedicated to deep fried fish. Here the ladies wear white gowns with matching hats, forever flipping their small, googly eyed offerings in wide pans of spitting black oil. The frenzied bubble and pop of the banks of deep fat fryers is so loud that all transactions have to be conducted in sign language.

Knowing my father he would have climbed higher still, to where frenzied commerce gives way to an older, more sedate La Paz. Here the Aymara women, known as *chollas* in their wide *pollera* skirts and bowler hats, sit contentedly amongst their open sacks of coca, spices, dried potato and grain. They truly are queens in their own silent kingdoms. The hectic pace of life in the rest of the city is in such contrast to the measured fullness of their time. La Paz has always been a city of traders and many of these *chollas* have been very successful. Some have built extravagant palaces in El Alto, visible beneficiaries of the Evo Morales years.

The lower end of Sagarnaga runs down into the bustling city centre, the barrio of Sopocachi and the Zona Sur beyond. The last time I ever saw Dad in South America was in the late 1990s in Sopochachi, when I was still living in La Paz. He was passing though on one of his many business trips from Rio, where he was living at the time. By this stage in his career he had long left fieldwork behind, working as the senior vice-president of exploration in South America for a multi-national mining company.

We met with a characteristically formal handshake (Dad wasn't one for emotional reunions) on a Sunday morning in the foyer of the Radisson Hotel in downtown La Paz. He looked well, tanned and handsome for his years in a pair of smart brown cords, a sweater over a pink shirt and a pair of polished brogues. Seldom out of a suit in his later working life he looked a bit awkward in casual dress.

From the Radisson it is a short walk to Plaza Avaroa, one of my favourite spots in the city's middle class district of Sopocachi. A huge bronze statue of a stricken man pointing indistinctly towards the horizon sits on a high plinth in the middle of the square. A dried-out fountain is supposed to be bathing his feet in perpetuity.

This is Edwardo Avaroa, fallen hero of the disastrous War of the Pacific in the 1880s, when Bolivia lost its coastal territory to Chile and with it the nation's connection to the sea. The loss is still keenly felt with local radio stations playing the sound of breaking waves to their land-locked listeners before reminding them that 'this should be yours.'

We sat on a grassy bank in front of the statue, soaking up the spring sunshine. The trees around the square had burst into life, throwing long, tangled shadows across our limbs. I felt the warmth penetrating my bones after a long winter of dry cold. I fetched us a couple of *choripan* from a nearby stall, chorizo style sausages served with a burning hot sauce in delicious crusty *maraceta* rolls.

We ate contentedly in silence for a while, listening to the murmur of a city in repose: children chattering on swings, an ice-cream vendor calling out '*helado, helado,*' the chime of a distant church bell. When he finally got round to catching up – you could never rush Dad into conversation – he seemed more relaxed than I usually found him on our often awkward encounters. We stuck to safe ground, talking about my work and life in La Paz, on the surface so unchanged since he first visited in 1976.

He told me a little more about this first trip, the beginning of his 25-year love affair with the Bolivian Altiplano. He remembered how walking into the witches' market back then felt like straying across an invisible line into a forbidden world in those days. If tourists so much as produced a camera they were pelted with stones.

In the evenings Dad hung out in the tourist bars and *peñas*, listening to folk music and chatting to other gringos. On one of these nocturnal sojourns he struck up a friendship with a Swiss explorer who was sailing around the world. Dad joined him on his yacht on his overland leg between the Pacific and the Atlantic, incongruously drinking cocktails as they were towed up La Paz's main drag, hundreds of miles from the sea.

From La Paz my father spent weeks studying copper deposits in the Cordillera Real on the border between Bolivia and Chile. He talked about the breathless exhilaration of his solitary fieldwork in the high Andes, and the magnetic draw that he had felt to the Altiplano ever since. Before Bolivia Dad had been working in the Eastern Highlands of Papua New Guinea where his exploration, restricted by the tree cover, was following mineral traces in the sediments of riverbeds. He longed for a clear line of site under the jungle's dense canopy, the sense of claustrophobia only amplified by the constant white noise of the rivers he had follow to avoid getting disorientated and lost.

In the high Andes dad's horizons were cut loose. With no vegetation he could scan the mountains and see their curves in billions of years of tectonic pressure and volcanic eruption. Much of his work was at the surface, scanning for rocks and interesting anomalies. He told me that interpreting the geology of a landscape is like a detective story with only a handful of clues. You only have the smallest pieces of a vast interlocking jigsaw in three dimensions to interpret.

This means that small finds can tell big stories, fantastical narratives. A 65 million year old shark's tooth could be from a sea-bed in the cretaceous period that has been lifted with tilting layers of pressured rock into the present day Andes. A particular sedimentary rock such as feldspar in an ancient river-bed could be the traces of a mountain range that has long since collapsed and died.

My father loved these mountains and spoke of them with a kind of reverence, a softly spoken spiritual association that stretched far beyond the science of his investigations. He once showed me pictures of their slopes, streaked with mineral deposits that flowed together in rusting iron oranges and copper greens. They looked to me like giant canvases, painted into being with bold brush stokes.

He would tell his beloved mountain's life stories and explain how geological time isn't just about its vast scale, far beyond the comprehension of human existence. Geological time's arrow flows simultaneously forward and back. Mountains are similar to us in having both life and death cycles. Like us their end is as important as their beginning. Although he would never have admitted it I think he understood that they are dynamic features of our planet and therefore, ultimately, living entities.

Our conversation meandered into some of the other wild and remote places he had spent time in as a young geologist. His years of adventure in the Star Mountains of Papua New Guinea, where I was born. Exploring the bone white beaches and deep forests of the Indonesian coastline. His long trips into the heart of the Amazon rainforest on motorised canoes. The time he spent surveying remote corners of Alaska, armed with a .303 rifle to fend off the Grizzlies.

I always loved these stories and would burst with pride that this man, however disconnected from my life, was my father. Even in the brogues and pink shirt he still looked to me every bit the adventurer that I had so idolised as a boy. As we leisurely timed out our last hours together I could see the bond shimmering between us, tremulous and fragile in the bright morning air.

As well as his core samples and textiles, Dad brought home one more clue from his time in La Paz back in the 70s. A diminutive plaster figure of a man with an impressive moustache and a manic, slack jawed grin that still sits on my desk. He is dressed in a brown suit with orange woolly hat and stands with his arms thrown wide open. Bags of grain and cereals hang from his waist and a handful of miniature hundred dollar bills are strung around his neck.

There is something unsettling, almost burlesque about this figure, like the compere at a circus act. I often wondered why Dad, who had exquisite taste in most things, had taken the trouble to bring this wee man all the way back to Scotland. I still quietly inherited him after my dad left home, even though his arm had been glued on at least once and a mouse had nibbled away at most of his grain. I felt duty bound to hang onto him because he had become oddly familiar, a reminder of my dad around the house.

It was only years later that I realised that this was no ordinary souvenir from Bolivia. Dad had in fact brought an Ekeko into our lives, La Paz's very own Aymara God of abundance. Every January the people of La Paz, known as *paceños*, flock to the Alasitas Festival to honour the Ekeko. By buying their material desires in miniature at the festival they hope that he will then grant them in real life over the coming year.

But there is a catch. For the magic to work you are supposed to take an idol of the Ekeko home and twice weekly ply him with cigarettes, coca leaves and alcohol. Failure to do so is punishable with a lifetime of ill fortune. So rather than a bizarre household ornament it turned out that I had actually inherited the equivalent of a vengeful pet that demands constant attention and can never be relegated to the attic or a bin.

Curious to revisit the festival that had brought the Ekeko into our family I had timed my flight into La Paz to catch the start of Alasitas. From my hotel in Sagarnaga the festival was only a short walk down town. I arrived to catch the atmosphere at night, just as the opening ceremony was ending. The musicians were still packing up their bags on stage and a cordon of heavily armed police was waiting for a local dignitary to emerge from the loo. The large crowd that had gathered for the speeches was now funnelling through the festival's narrow portal into a jumbled alleyways of stalls that ran down the hill below.

Before I even reached the first stall I had been offered $10,000 dollars in crisp notes, a law degree from the University of San Andres and a Bolivian passport. I couldn't resist becoming a Bolivian national for around 10 pence. The three-inch burgundy passport came with a 'gold visa,' airline ticket, banker's draft and five one hundred dollars neatly stapled to the back.

It took a moment to adjust to the Alasitas economy of scale, where the whole world is sold off in miniature. There were brightly painted cars, houses, desktop computers, fridges, furniture and tools, all no larger than the palm of my hand. The packets of detergent, soap, cereal, rice, tea, coffee and cigarettes were even smaller, each meticulously decorated with popular brand names like Quaker Oats and Lux soap.

It isn't just material desires that this festival caters for. I stopped to watch a man behind one stall peering through a magnifying glass to name, sign and stamp a miniature graduation certificate for an aspiring Law student. He also offered driving licences, land ownership deeds and rental agreements. I felt humbled that these were the sum of most Bolivians' wildest desires. Most of what they hope for I have grown up taking for granted.

Despite the festival's urban crowd and gaudy commerce there was a distinctly pagan flavour to proceedings. The air was thick with smoky incense from the charcoal burners of the festival's witch doctors. They sat patiently on woven blankets, ready to bless each small purchase with white spirit, petals and prayers. Some offered to tell peoples fortunes with coca leaves, cards and bubbling pots of molten tin.

And there was the idol of the Ekeko himself. He came in all shapes and sizes, ranging from an incense stick holder to the full-blown clay figure that Dad had brought home. These modern versions looked no less menacing to my eye than the one that I had left in Scotland. I resolved to give mine a tot of whisky, cigarette and a pat on the back as soon as I got home.

Luckily there was plenty to distract a guilty conscience. Alasitas is as much a fun fair as a street market and was packed with kids playing table football, riding lethal looking fairground rides and exploring the tent full of bendy mirrors. I stepped into a small booth to have my portrait taken in front of a lush backdrop of the Iguaçu falls. The photographer insisted I wear a white tracksuit top and matching baseball cap to give the impression that I was actually there. He was even kind enough to digitally enhance the colours to give me a bright orange, tropical tan, for added authenticity. The resulting photo was truly astounding.

In the late afternoon a thunderstorm broke over the city and everyone dashed for cover from a torrent of hailstones. I stood under the awning of a makeshift café selling a sticky maize drink called *api* served in a tall glass and accompanied by a fluffy pastry. The drink is hot and sweet with a similar consistency to pinhead porridge. Much more palatable looking were the long trails of *churros* bubbling away in oil in the next-door stall. I watched them being rescued with a slotted spoon, deftly cut to size and neatly coiled in paper bags with a dusting of icing sugar.

The hailstones on the corrugated tin roof above me hammered out an irregular rhythm as stallholders lit candles and lanterns for the night shift ahead. The sky above was peat black and the steep valley's sides now bristled with electric light. The lady in the stall opposite had pinned a white sheet across her entire display to protect it from the hail. I watched the light from a candle within dance her shadow across the sheet and wondered at the magic of this Andean city that so held my father in its thrall.

Did my Dad, the learned scientist, have a momentary lapse of reason at the Alasitas all those years ago? He didn't just visit the festival, a must for tourists to this day. He went out of his way to buy an Ekeko and must have felt compelled by collective superstition to transport it all the way home to the other side of the world. I imagined him tucking the dainty package under his arm all those years ago, worried about bumping into a fellow geologist with it on the street. I'll never know what he wished for, or if there was a price to pay at the crossroads.

Most travellers to the Altiplano get properly hit by altitude sickness, known locally as *sorojche*, within 24 hours of reaching the city. On my first wander around the city centre I found the 50 yard uphill walk back to my hostel demanded immense mental endurance and stamina. I had to stop several times to catch my breath and at one point endured the humiliation of being overtaken by an old Aymara man bent double with a sofa on his back. Other than a hit of Oxyshot, the cure all is coca tea. Although much maligned as the principle ingredient in cocaine, the coca leaf is integral to Aymara culture as well as a cure all for *sorojche*.

But Bolivia has another lurking baptism of fire. My downfall was almost immediate as I couldn't resist a plateful of *Anticucho*, one of my favourite La Paz delicacies at the Alasitas festival. This is definitely street food for the hardy of stomach: sliced heart of cow, flambéed in petrol and washed down with a spicy peanut sauce. The Aymara ladies or *cholas* who man the BBQs shoot up theatrical sheets of flame with petrol doused rags to draw in passing trade.

But moments of sensory indulgence like this rarely come alone. 'It is something everyone who comes here has to go through,' the waitress informed me in the hotel café days later. The soothing plate of rice with chicken that she served (the first solids to pass my lips in 48 hours) barely paused inside to take in the view. Stuck in La Paz, my plans to catch a night bus to Potosi were put on hold indefinitely.

In desperation I decided on an expedition to the local pharmacy. Most Bolivians can't afford a doctor when they get ill, so they go directly to the drug dispensary for both diagnosis and cure. The pharmacists take their elevated role seriously. They openly discuss the intimate details of their patients ailments, often in front of interested fellow customers, before dispensing hard-core drugs with alarming alacrity. The cure-all for these modern day apothecaries is usually a massive dose of antibiotics, which as luck would have it was just what I needed.

I managed to stagger down to the local pharmacy, a tiny shop brimming with high shelves of potions and pills, only to find it completely deserted. A sign by the till advertised the 'Gigantic and Super Potent Penis Max.' I guessed from the sales pitch that Viagra had finally made it to the Altiplano.

I leant forward to see a bald man in a white coat crouched behind the counter, studiously pumping a blood pressure monitor strapped around his own arm. On noticing me he leaped up like a jack-in-the-box and politely asked, as though nothing was out of the ordinary, just how he could be of help. We both chose to ignore the embarrassing hiss of his gently deflating armband.

Diagnosis was perfunctory. 'What you need my friend,' he told me on hearing of my symptoms, 'is a very strong dose of *antibioticas.*' With an air of hushed ceremony he produced one red and one blue pill, each the size of a large cough sweet. Stepping back for effect he held up a pill in each hand. 'First you must take the red one,' he told me. 'Then you must take this blue one immediately afterwards,' he added, arching one eyebrow for effect.

There was a long pause as he stood there holding up the two pills. It looked like he was expecting a round of applause. 'Why do I have to take the blue pill?' I asked hurriedly, sensing that my window of opportunity was fast closing before the next scheduled touchdown with a toilet seat. 'To prevent the red pill from lacerating your stomach,' he answered, smiling reassuringly. 'Just watch out for some intense dreams my friend.'

Back at the hostel I forced the two pills down, half expecting to be dead by the morning. But the man in white was a medical magician after all, my very own hippocratic Willie Wonka. Back in my room I almost immediately started to feel better.

I lay on my bed and watched La Paz dissolve into night like the view through a window patterned with rain. The light is so physical here. It seems to disintegrate into particles, like silver flecks on an old black and white photo. It scatters like beads of mercury into shadows, leaving only the imprint of the city behind.

When I finally fell into a fitful sleep I drifted into a silent universe of stars. As I descended the pinpricks of light glowed neon and turned into street lights, illuminating a jumbled maze of roads and houses. Women in bowler hats sat over wide pans of tar black oil. Stray dogs emerged to eat rubbish – some dressed in old T-shirts to keep out the cold. I tried to escape but the further I fled down the streets the narrower and steeper they become. I turned into a blind alleyway. Spiders leapt at my bare legs out of the shadows. I picked my way through cobblestones covered with shit and old brushes.

And there at the road's end was an old man, waiting for me in front of a high brick wall. Although he stood expectantly, as straight as a rod, his frail body looked like a wire hanger under a baggy, brown suit. He wore a trilby that cast his high angular Andean features into deep shadow. As I approached ancient hands held out a dog – eared, paperback book.

But I couldn't tear my attention away from this man's inscrutable expression. His eyes glinted at me like hard struck flints; piercing, inquisitive and oddly indifferent. There was something familiar in those eyes as his face softened. Looking down I saw he was offering me a copy of Coriolanus.

I woke to the sound of gunfire. At least that is what it sounded like as I gingerly edged open the balcony doors to another salvo of blasts outside. The street was filled with cordite and colour, the cries of the street sellers competing with the thunderous report of protesters' fireworks ricocheting around the valley. Hundreds of marchers were streaming down Sagarnaga towards Plaza San Francisco in front of the cathedral, a rallying point for the country's backdrop of constant political turmoil and social unrest.

The plaza itself had been transformed into the sort of carnival parade you would expect before a big football match. At the centre was a thirty-foot blow up representation of the country's longstanding president Evo Morales. The balloon figure resembled a cross between Super Mario without the moustache and an oversized sex doll. It looked like it had seen a fair amount of electioneering action and swayed menacingly over a group of pan pipers with a deflated lilt.

But nothing was going to puncture the crowd's ardour. Waving the rainbow coloured *Wiphala* flags that represent Bolivia's 36 indigenous 'nations,' they carried large banners at the front that boldly stated '*Evo Para Siempre*' or '*La Revolucion Continua!*' and set the sky alight with a constant barrage of hand-held pyrotechnics.

How times have changed. When my father was in La Paz back in 1976 a street protest like this would have been met with a hail of gunfire. Coups in Uruguay and Chile in 1973 ushered in a 'Southern Cone Model' of dictatorship in South America, characterised by the prohibition of union activity, free market economics and brutal military rule. Most repressive of all was Pinochet's Chile and the string of Argentine military rulers from 1976 who tortured and disappeared tens of thousands of civilians in their 'Dirty War' against the communists, intellectuals, the 'enemy within.'

The Bolivia that Dad visited was then in the grip of the military dictatorship of Colonel Hugo Banzer Suárez. Although Banzer's rule from January 1970 until 1978 was not as extreme as his friend Pinochet's he still closed universities, radios and newspapers and reinstated the death penalty. Opposition activists were dealt a heavy hand by the military and branded 'subversives' or 'Castro-communists'. Any direct threat to Banzer's authority was crushed by the army.

Most notorious of all was the 'massacre of the valley' outside of Cochabamba only two years before Dad jetted into La Paz. When farmers or *campesinos* set up road blocks in January 1974 to protest against the withdrawal of subsidies on basic goods they were mowed down by tanks and fighter jets. Anywhere between 80 and 200 corpses were spirited away to mass graves in army trucks.

Bolivia's political history since Spanish rule has been a dismal narrative of massacres, corruption and cock-ups. There were 193 coups – most of them violent – between the country's independence from Spain in 1825 and 1982. Nine Bolivian presidents in all have been assassinated, five of them while still in office. In 1946 President Villarroel was physically dragged out of the presidential palace in La Paz by an angry mob and hanged from a lamp-post in Plaza Murillo.

Much of the blame for almost 200 years of political instability lies with the country's political elite. After independence a long line of swaggering strong men, known as *caudillos,* continued to exploit Bolivia's indigenous majority for cheap labour and taxes, rather than build an inclusive nation state. Their attitude is best summed up by the old Bolivian saying; 'the stupid ones work and the clever ones live off the stupid.'

The career of president Mariano Melgarejo is a fairly extreme example of Bolivia's political class. He literally shot to power by putting a bullet though Isidoro Belzu's chest at his rival's presidential inauguration in 1864. Melgarejo then appeared at the balcony of the palace and shouted to the crowd that had gathered to welcome Belzu: 'Belzu is dead, who lives now?' 'Vive Melgarejo!' the crowd obediently chanted their reply.

Melgarejo's seven-year stint in power was marked by territorial losses and the appropriation of indigenous community land. In 1867 he ceded 300,000 sq km of Bolivian territory to Brazil in return for the gift of a white horse. He is reputed to have delineated the boundary for this gift by galloping his new horse over a large map of his country and tracing out the section that its hoof landed on.

Foreign policy certainly wasn't Melgarejo's strong point. On one drunken night in 1870 he called his troops from their garrison and led them out of La Paz on a forced march to defend Paris from a German besieging army in the Prussian war. When told by one of his generals that they would never make it across the Atlantic, Melgarejo reportedly shouted: 'Don't be stupid! We can take short cut through the bush.'

The disfranchised Aymara and Quechua peoples of the Altiplano have responded to Bolivia's seemingly endless misrule with intense bouts of resistance and the odd outright rebellion. The greatest single insurrection during the colonial period was the siege of La Paz by the Aymara leader Tupac Katari in 1781. Commanding the heights of El Alto, Katari and his rebel army blocked all routes into the city for 109 days. Deprived of supplies, over 10,000 *paceños*, one third of the city's population, starved to death.

Katari and his wife Bartolina Sisa mocked their oppressors at night, dancing in fine clothes, eating with silver knives and forks, and assuming Spanish names. Eventually outgunned, Katari's revolt was crushed. Katari himself was tied to four white horses ripped limb from limb. Before he died he said that he had lit a candle that could not be extinguished, and promised: 'When I return I will be millions.'

By as late as 1952 a strict system of racial segregation was still in place in La Paz, with indigenous citizens prevented from voting, or even entering Plaza Murillo. I have a Bolivian friend who admitted that his grandfather would beat any '*indio*' with his walking staff who dared to step off the road and onto the pavement.

A violent revolution in 1952 brought some hope. Led by a radicalised group of middle class intellectuals, the *Movimiento National Revolucionario* (MNR) party introduced universal suffrage, improved workers rights and redistributed land. But the MNRs reforming zeal was soon driven into the sand, overtaken by corruption, self-interest and the long arm of Uncle Sam.

The extremes between rich and poor were so marked in Bolivia that the country caught the attention of the Cuban revolutionary Che Guevara and right hand man to Fidel Castro. Che smuggled himself into the country in 1966 and set up a small camp in the jungle outside Santa Cruz which he hoped to use as a springboard for Marxist revolution across the continent. But his grand ambitions were short lived. Although the mines were hotbeds of political dissent President Barrientos still commanded considerable support in the countryside where Guevara was hiding out. Increasingly isolated, Che was eventually hunted down with help from the CIA, and executed in the remote hamlet of La Higuera in October 1967.

When I turned up in Bolivia in 1997 to work as a journalist the same Hugo Banzer had bizarrely returned to shore up his legacy as the new democratically elected president and head of the right leaning ADN party. Keen to smooth over the misdeeds of his past, the reformed Banzer presented himself as a wise and compassionate patriarch. I worked with others to shine light on his past, referring to him as the former dictator and writing stories about 'Operation Condor' – the alleged shadowy exchange of political prisoners for torture between Argentina, Chile and Bolivia during Banzer's rule in the 1970s. The national magazine that I wrote the article for was mysteriously broken into just before the day before it was was due to be distributed. Every copy was stolen and the article never saw the light of day.

What shocked me most about reporting on Bolivian politics was the endemic corruption. It seemed like everyone within the ruling classes was in some way on the take with nepotism and cronyism rife. One surreal experience I had when trying to chase up an interview with a still prominent politician sums it up. I took these notes at the time:

"The door opens, or rather I open it. Inside is a tidy room. There is a hat rack by the waste paper bin, a suit jacket folded neatly over the chair in the corner. There is a newspaper on the table, carefully laid out so that it can be turned without creasing. Behind the desk sits a small man with glasses and a neatly clipped beard. He has his hands splayed out on the table edge in front of him and his fingernails are immaculate. He is Don Pablo's secretary, only Don Pablo no longer works here. He politely informs me that I

have the wrong address and Don Pablo has
moved to new offices in parliament. He goes on
to admit that he has long since been left behind.
And so he sits, from nine to five, reading the
paper and sipping the occasional mate de coca in
this box room. He takes his salary every month
knowing that as long as he sits quietly in this
room his shadow job is secure."

With power so corrupted the centre could not hold forever. I remember turning on the BBC news back home in Scotland in 2003 and being horrified by footage of protesters facing down tanks, teargas and machinegun fire in La Paz. The final trigger for revolt was the discovery of huge natural gas fields in the eastern lowlands, second only to Venezuela's in the entire continent. At the mercy of economic policies imposed by the IMF and World Bank in exchange for loans, foreign companies signed lucrative contracts with the Government of Gonzalo Sanchez de Lozada to siphon gas profits out of the country. Meanwhile 35% of the nation continued to survive on less than $1 per day.

Just as poverty in this 'resource rich' nation deepened, so did its people's sense of injustice. Protests spilled over into open rebellion when the word got out that the Government planned to export gas via Bolivia's old enemy, Chile. It was enough that Bolivians powerful neighbour had 'stolen' their access to the sea in the 1879 – 1884 War of the Pacific. It now looked like they were being handed the glittering prize of cheap energy on a silver platter by their very own president.

The citizens of El Alto blocked all the roads going into La Paz. Youths hauled trains off tracks with their bare hands, pushing them onto the highway to stop the military and police from entering the city. Bunkered into his palace the President sent in trigger-happy troops from the eastern city of Santa Cruz to crush the siege. Despite the death of 69 civilians in 24 hours of indiscriminate violence, the people of El Alto – backed by protesters across the country – held their nerve. Sanchez de Lozada, unrepentant to the end, flew out of the country and into exile, the old political order crumbling behind him.

Into the vacuum stepped Evo Morales. The son of a llama herder, this charismatic leader from humble origins was elected Bolivia's first indigenous president in 2006. His incorporation as both the county's democratic president and the supreme leader of the Aymara kingdom marked the symbolic end of 500 years of virtual slavery at the hands of both the Spanish and the independent republic that followed.

Evo's first election back in 2006 ushered in a remarkable period of economic growth and political stability for a country so used to protest and trauma. Under Evo's self-styled Plural-National state the gap between rich and poor has shrunk markedly with extreme poverty in the country shrinking from 35% to 13% since he took office. Public infrastructure projects have also delivered improved roads and a new airport as well as La Paz's awesome cable car system.

Bolivia was once famous for having, according to the UN, the world's most dangerous road. The slender ribbon of track which ran from La Paz to Coroico in the semi-tropical Yungas was hewn into a vertical cliff and frequently blocked by landslides. To pass oncoming traffic you had to take the outside line on the descent with passengers nervously watching the wheels inch towards the cliff edge, shouting warnings if the bus got too close.

The drivers themselves knew the risks all too well, stopping at the Cumbre or highest point to make offerings of coca and raw alcohol to the *Pachamama* for safe passage. Many still ended up going over the edge, with hundreds of passengers killed every year. I remember seeing a big bus, one I would have caught if I had made it to the station an hour earlier, upturned far below. It was only a glimpse but I saw bodies thrown from it and people searching the corpses and the wreckage for valuables.

Now 'The Death Road' is a catchy phrase to attract travellers looking for adventure. Closed to traffic it has become an exhilarating downhill bike ride that puts fate firmly in your hands rather than a driver. Tour groups have made it a right of passage on the gringo trail. On the other side of the valley Evo's government has built a brand new road for cars and buses into the Yungas that is largely asphalted, two-lanes and saves hundreds of lives every year.

But for all his achievements Evo's overall record has, perhaps inevitably, been a mixed one. Critics point to the high costs of development in the country's natural resources with national parks like Madidi opened up to oil and gas exploration and the violent repression of the Tipnis indigenous group for opposing a new road through their ancestral lands in the Chapare. Little has been done to tackle endemic corruption in the public sector and even many of Evo's most avid supporters question why he has built so many football pitches all over the country rather than hospitals.

Nowhere is this more evident than in La Paz were the new government building, *Casa Grande del Pueblo* or the Grand House of the People, which dominates the historic city centre skyline. Built with public funds in a city that is seriously lacking in health and education infrastructure, the 29-storey skyscraper has become a controversial symbol of Evo's long tenure in Bolivian politics. Having said that, there's no denying that the lobby with its brilliantly coloured representation of the country's 36 indigenous groups, painted by the acclaimed artist Mamani Mamani, is a bold and fresh take on Bolivian national identity.

Once idolised in the West as the darling of the left, Evo appears to be losing interest in democracy. In fact some argue that he is now clinging on to power as fiercely as some of the old school *caudillos* he supposedly swept aside. His party *Movimiento al Socialismo* (MAS) has changed the constitution to allow him to run for an unprecedented fourth presidential term in 2019, despite narrowly losing a referendum on the matter back in 2016. He is likely to win again, although public opinion is sharply divided between supporters who want Evo to 'finish what he has started,' and those who believe his mandate has long overrun its course.

Whatever the fate of Morales it does now feel as though Katari's millions have returned. It is hard to imagine Bolivia slipping back to the bad old days of rule by a white elite with a narrow neo-liberal agenda, or the dictatorships of the past. Bolivia is an increasingly proud and confident Andean nation with political representation as fractured and diverse as its geography and complex make up. Social movements have to jostle to make their demands heard and although corruption is still rife the old post-colonial order has for now lost its grip.

As the evening wore on the protest in Plaza San Francisco disintegrated into a quintessentially Bolivian night out. The grand finale of fireworks was set off in the middle of the crowd, quickly clearing the plaza of supporters in a mushroom of smoke and falling sparks. The panpipers from Potosi were too drunk to play a coherent tune and a scuffle broke out between two men who both wanted to wave the same flag.

Superficially I imagined that little had changed since my father first walked up Sagarnaga back in the 1970s. But it still felt as though I had stepped into a different country to the one he first visited all those years ago.

POTOSI

The night bus from the central station in La Paz to Potosí was humming with activity long before we pulled out. Aymara women clambered aboard and bustled down the narrow aisle with plastic bags dripping with fried chicken and large saucepans of hot tea. An old man stepped up, arms laden with glistening silver chains and handed them around for us to feel and try on 'without obligation' before recovering them. Many street vendors make their living from weary passengers, stocking up on provisions and presents for distant family members before the long haul into dawn.

The street children were the true performers. A boy stood at the front and woodenly recited a few jokes before blessing us all on our journey and asking for 'a small appreciation.' Two cheeky brothers with baseball caps worn back to front sang snatches of a love song in harmony. They quickly lost interest and switched to an impromptu rap song about how the bus driver may be fat but was hung like a horse. He threw them off and ground the bus into motion.

The bus started the long crawl up the *autopista* towards El Alto. Just as we were settling into the comfortable anonymity of our journey a portly man in a cheap suit jumped up from his seat and launched into a lengthy sales pitch about the incredible healing properties of the Andean root *maca*. Bolivians like to start any public address with a lengthy thank you in flowery Spanish and this occasion was no exception.

'Ladies and gentlemen,' he boomed, 'first of all I would like to offer my most profound thanks to the driver for giving me the opportunity to share this time with you. I would also like to thank you graciously for your patience and interest in the important message I have for you today.'

This wasn't even the warm up for the main act. 'A special thanks to the bus company which is transporting you with comfort and safety to your final destination,' he added. 'I would also like to thank my sponsors, who have given me the opportunity to support myself and my family by selling this product that also has immeasurable health benefits for your family.'

I half expected him to go on and thank his mother for bringing him into the world, the world for providing an environment conducive to life and the universe for cradling the world in its starry bosom.

He then opened a folder to reveal a series of graphic images of naked people suffering from morbid obesity, arthritis, cancer and bizarre genital deformities. These are, he kindly explained, all the result of a bad diet and could be prevented by a teaspoon of his miraculous root plant powder every morning.

He went on to tip a small amount of this powder onto the palms of our hands from a bright sachet, 'yours today for only two dollars, three for the price of four.' It had the texture of sawdust and didn't taste much better.

Having made a few sales our man jumped off at El Alto's city limits. I peered into the gloom that quickly enveloped him but the pavement was absorbed in rain swept darkness. A street on the outskirts of El Alto is empty ground waiting to be built on. There is seldom running water or electricity and you only have to walk to the tidemark of plastic rubbish beyond the last adobe house to reach the open country of the Altiplano.

The driver's assistant finally managed to get the tracking straight on the TV an hour into the trip and a music video spluttered into life of four ageing *latino* men with astonishing mullets, singing a power ballad about frustrated love. I kept my attention firmly fixed on the infinite blackness outside. Driving through these thinning lands at night must feel similar to sailing across the icy seas of the Southern Ocean. With no artificial lights or rising land the view out of the window is of the cosmos, perfectly cocooned in velvety darkness. The Southern Cross points the way south, to the continent's end and Antarctica beyond.

I tried to imagine the great mule and llama caravans, hundreds of animals strong that would have trekked across this same ground in the colonial period. The city of Potosí was built out of the Altiplano's parched earth and had to import virtually all of its commodities. Grain was transported from Cochabamba to the east; hides, dried meat and fish from what is now Chile to the west; pack animals, salt, sugar, wine and textiles from Argentina in the south. Even fuel, in the form of wood and dung, had to be carried in from the surrounding areas to combat the cold and fire the silver furnaces.

The caravans from La Paz carried all number of goods including hot chillies and fresh fruit from the tropical lowlands, dried llama meat known as *charque* and the freeze dried potatoes or *chuño* that are so typical of the region. Mercury, used from the 1570s to extract silver, was even transported by mule in crudely fashioned hide containers from mines on the far side of Lake Titicaca.

The biggest cargo of all was dried coca leaves from the slopes of the Andes. The Spanish initially derided the leaves for their importance in Incan religion, but coca's crucial role in the mines quickly overcame their misgivings. When chewed the coca leaf is a natural appetite suppressor and provider of sustained energy at high altitudes. Coca allowed the silver miners to work for long hours on very little nutrition.

It would have taken these herdsmen and traders several weeks to cover the six hundred kilometres between La Paz and Potosí. Blinded by the high Andean sun during the day and frozen at night, the Altiplano's flat monotony must have been the hardest to bear on this gruelling trek. The only visual break in the journey would have been the shimmering haze of Lake Poopó with its flocks of pink flamingos and circular pre-Columbian tombs that dot the shoreline.

I know the strangeness of this landscape well, having travelled out to a tiny Aymara village to stay with a British friend years earlier. He was there to carry out his field research for an anthropology degree but was having a spot of bother with the locals. Apart from the village elder who had invited him to stay no-one wanted to participate in his study, let alone talk to him. By the time I reached him his sanity was being preserved by a long wire aerial to the BBC World Service.

To distract him from the relentless sunshine and solitude I suggested a day's walk to the nearby Lake Poopó, around 1,000 square kilometers of saline water 3,680 meters above sea level. Only it wasn't as near as it looked. In fact it was an optical illusion, a shimmering oasis in the heat that seemed to recede the longer we walked towards it though the Altiplano desert. By the time we reached its shore, dotted with the stone funerary towers or *chullpas* of long lost cultures, we realised the waters had receded. We navigated several hundred metres of mud caked flats before finally reaching the actual lake.

The flamingos were spectacular, their ruffled plumage rippling in the lake's milky green surface. They call many of the lakes in the southern Altiplano *'lagunas coloradas'* because of the mineral deposits that paint them vivid greens and reds. Andean, Chilean and the endangered James Flamingos flock to them to feed off the microscopic crustations in the mud. It is so cold at this altitude in the winter that they have to wait patiently every morning for the ice to defrost around their spindly legs and set them free.

We had to turn around pretty smartly as we had already spent the best part of the day getting there and our water supplies were getting low. On the way back hunger got the better of me and I reluctantly tucked into the pasta and sheep brain salad in plastic tupperware that the village elder had kindly made for our walk. I still vividly remember the translucent box packed tight with sweating pasta, the slippery sensation as it slid down my throat and the flecks of grey matter. My friend, who knew better than to touch his piece, cackled like the mad Scotsman he is while I vomited it all straight back up again.

Only now do I realise that those shrinking shores were an omen that Lake Poopo was dying. Contamination from mining together with poor water management on the Desaguadero river to irrigate increased quinoa plantations had already sickened the lake. But evaporation accelerated dramatically as the mean temperature in the area increased by 0.9 degrees Celsius between 1995 and 2005 alone.

In 2014 the water disappeared entirely and tens of thousands of fish died in the mud, the stench hanging in the air for weeks. To this day all that remains are some marshy patches. Although the lake has dried up completely before, scientists say this time round it is unlikely ever to recover. The melting of Andean glaciers means there simply isn't enough available fresh water to replenish it.

The Uru-Murato people in and around the community of Llapallapani have been the hardest hit. The oldest indigenous group in the region, they lived on floating islands made of reeds and dressed in clothes made by hand from feathers and wool until they decided to settle on the lake shores. Known in the area as simply as 'the people of the lake' the men spent as long as two weeks at a time expertly navigating the lake's winds and currents in small wooden boats, in pursuit of schools of sardine sized Karachi and bigger Pejerrey.

The Uru-Murato have also long supplemented their diet with meat from the flocks of Flamingos that frequented Lake Poopo. They used mirrors to cast sunlight into their eyes and temporarily lull them into sleep. The birds also served to help with common ailments. The pink fat was used to alleviate rheumatism and the feathers to help relieve fevers.

Having weathered Incan and Spanish conquests the Uru-Murato have never faced a challenge like this. Their lake has vanished and with no fishing many are forced to travel huge distances to work in lead mines or on the salt flats. Once proud fishermen in charge of their own destiny they are now forced into manual labor up to 200 miles from their homes. Many more have joined the global throng of migrant peoples robbed by climate change. Under sustained pressure their communities are now dwindling and only a few hundred are thought to remain in Llapallapani and the neighboring villages.

A blast of arctic air woke me suddenly from my slumber. The bus had stopped and the door swung open. 'Break' the driver barked before jumping out. It was midnight and we were at the crossroads of an Altiplano outpost, made up of low adobe houses and a few pale orange streetlights.

I stumbled with my fellow sleepwalkers into a simple café, brightly lit with neon strips. The town was obviously the mid-way stopping point between several destinations and was well prepared for our nocturnal visit. We were served a piece of bread with a slice of cheese on a blue plastic plate and a cup of sweet black tea in a white tin mug. The cheese had curled at the edges from having sat out for hours, perhaps days. It tasted of salt.

Outside dogs began to gather in the electric light in the hope of scraps. Buses pulled up from different destinations to disgorge their equally groggy occupants. A group of blond Canadians in skater shorts travelling from the salt flats of Uyuni huddled together and smoked cigarettes. A team of teenage football players from Cochabamba in black shell suits carried on their boisterous banter from the changing room back home. The rest of us stood in our own little world near the bus, waiting for the driver to finish his beer and get back on the road.

It dawned on me that I had finally arrived at the Holy Grail of all travellers – somewhere in the middle of nowhere. It was one of those random nexuses, a meeting point of sorts where different lives connect, cross and separate. The only thing we all shared was a sense of disorientation, exhaustion and fear of having to visit the toilets. But somehow it found a common point in all our subconscious, a nameless town at night, a marker point for countless journeys.

Most people arrive in Potosí at dawn, raw and cold on the night bus from La Paz or Cochabamba. At six o'clock in the morning the first light had just seeped into the horizon beyond the city and the street lights, old Victorian style lanterns with electric bulbs, were still switched on. The town itself was made up of silhouettes and shadows. Colonial houses leaned into narrow streets with high wooden balconies. Ancient terracotta roofs bowed to mirror the emerging mountains and a sliver of moon hung in the sky like a shard of reflected glass.

Built more than 4,090 metres above sea level Potosí is one of the highest cities in the world. This unique setting, together with the crumbling Spanish architecture, gives it an atmosphere of haunted elegance. The surrounding landscape is unforgiving; a barren moonscape of sculptured rock, shaped by a relentless cycle of harsh sunlight, bitter cold and ferocious winds. And yet the town itself, with its grand balconies and heraldic shields, hints at a time of opulence and excess.

A dark mountain loomed imperiously over the city in the morning's crisp air. It could only be the Cerro Rico, the rich hill, with its near perfect conical symmetry. Only the hill's summit was illuminated by the dawn's diluted orange sun, revealing denuded, pockmarked slopes of red rock and grey mineral tailings. A ghostly trail of truck lights snaked off its midriff – miners coming home from the night shift. The Cerro Rico, the very reason for Potosí's existence, remained cloaked to me in its many aliases; the beautiful hill, the king of hills, the hill that has wept, the mountain that eats men.

According to local legend a native Quechua man Diego Huallpa was herding his flock of llamas around the Cerro Rico one evening in 1545 when one of them escaped up onto the mountain. He went looking for it only to be caught out by the quickly setting sun and was forced to find shelter in a cave where he lit a fire to survive the night's intense cold. Looking up at the cave's roof he saw a vein of pure silver illuminated by the flames. One legend claims that a stream of molten silver trickled out from under his fire.

The silver didn't stop flowing. For over two hundred years after Huallpa's discovery the Cerro Rico yielded over half of the world's production of silver. It was said that you could build a narrow bridge from the entrance of the Cerro Rico to the Escorial in Spain with all of the silver that poured out of it. This may be fanciful but the quantities were staggering. Between 1503 and 1660 some sixteen thousand tons of silver arrived in the Spanish port of Sanlúcar de Barrrameda from the Americas alone.

The Cerro Rico was the Spanish Empire's El Dorado, although the city that flourished at its foothills was paved with silver rather than gold. Potosí's streets between the principal cathedral and the church of Recoleta were actually resurfaced with silver bars for the Corpus Christi celebrations of 1658. At the time something of great value was said to be '*vale un Potosí*,' worth a Potosí.

I felt a tightening in my stomach and shortness of breath before we even get off the bus. At first I thought it was the body shock of reaching over four thousand metres. And then I realised that I felt trapped here. Trapped by the maze of interconnected alleys and streets. Trapped in a city that will never escape its at once splendid and terrible past.

The big wooden doors to the Hostel Carlos V were still firmly closed by nine o'clock in the morning. I leaned hard on the buzzer, fed up with waiting in the plaza for someone to open up. I had been sitting on a park bench with a clutch of slumbering pigeons at my feet since the bus arrived three hours earlier.

Eventually there was a jangle of keys, accompanied by some indistinguishable muttering of protest. A short, plump woman in her mid forties with a shock of frizzy hair and big, sad eyes opened the door in her nightgown. I told her that I had made a reservation by phone from La Paz but she seemed unimpressed, pausing for a long moment before finally stepping aside to let me in.

Doña Marta was the proprietor of Hostel Carlos V, described in my guidebook as a 'charmingly converted colonial house with simple but clean rooms looking onto a glass-roofed central patio.' I had imagined sitting on a white balcony overlooking a profusion of flowers, drinking beer to the light patter of rain overhead.

Instead the high glass ceiling in the gloomy central courtyard was so dirty that it only let in a thin, diffused light. The pink walls were faded and newspapers had been laid out on the wooden floors, presumably to save on polishing. I was shown to a dark room with a bed that had sunk into the same contours of the last guest who slumbered there. Doña Marta charged me double for the privilege of plugging in my laptop and told me I would be able to write in peace because

I was her only guest. 'Some comfort' I though to myself.

'It is the low season in Potosí,' she went on to tell me, 'there just aren't any tourists.' But her excuses didn't add up. I had already seen plenty of travellers drifting around looking for somewhere to stay, or for a decent feed. I soon realised that Doña Marta refused to take groups because of the 'inconvenience' and locked the front door whenever she was out, leaving potential guests languishing for hours at a time on the cold steps outside.

As Doña Marta took down my passport details I noticed a portrait of a young beauty above her desk. The girl's low cut velvet dress revealed a glittering sapphire necklace nestled into an impressive cleavage. Jet-black hair fell in loose curls around her bare shoulders and her almond shaped eyes shone out at me with a beguiling mix of innocence and mischief.

'Beautiful, isn't she' Doña Marta said holding out my passport, 'that was me, a very long time ago.' Only the shape of the eyes gave the two women away as the same person. Her hostel was a project that had long lost heart. Doña Marta admitted that she was fed up with changing beds and couldn't find a cleaner to help.

'All the people in Potosí that wanted to work have left for Argentina where they can make more money,' she said. 'I am going to put a sign saying closed for renovation,' she added. We laughed like fellow conspirators.

Nothing beats holing up in an anonymous hotel room, listening to the buzz of a foreign city that has no hold over you. I lay on my bed tracing the course of the cracks in the ceiling, wondering why Doña Marta had come to live here so alone. Why had an air of mournful neglect come to hang over her hostel, so grandly named after the Holy Roman Emperor and King of Spain between 1519 and 1556.

The place seemed to perfectly mirror its surrounds. Potosí has twenty-five remaining ornate churches and convents, as well as grand government buildings and colonial houses with the Spanish names still proudly carved into heraldic shields above the doors. *'I am rich Potosí, treasure of the world, king of mountains, envy of kings,'* reads the inscription on one. It seemed a hollow testament to distant times. This city's spirit of youth, vigor and optimism had long since departed.

As I sat in the central square an elderly woman in rags shuffled over to me trailing a mangy dog with matted hair and a weeping eye. She gave me her dog Bravo's life story as he puffed heavily at her side.

'I saved him many years ago after he was almost killed in a fight,' she told me, stroking him lovingly. 'Look at his eye, he is still blind from that day,' she added. 'I love Bravo like a son, he looks out for me, we are never apart.'

She pulled an intricately engraved antique silver dessert spoon from her shawl and offered it to me. 'Buy this from me,' she pleaded, 'I need food for me and Bravo.'

The delicately wrought spoon lay bright in my hand. This little reminder of past riches was now up for exchange to feed an old lady and her dog in Potosí, the poorest of towns in one of South America's poorest countries. Around 40% of Bolivia's population live below the poverty line with 13% surviving on less than 3.2 dollars a day. Just where had all the Cerro Rico's riches gone?

I figured that the colonial fortress skirting the plaza where we sat held some of the answers. The city's royal mint, the *Casa Real de la Moneda*, looks like a prison from the outside. Metal grilles on the windows cast tangled shadows over the building's high alabaster walls. It was here that up to six thousand coins a day were pressed for almost three hundred years until the Mint was finally closed in 1952. Today it is home to a rambling museum dedicated to the city's past.

I walked through the Mint's front entrance to find it virtually deserted. Two security men in green quilted jackets paced out their shift in the courtyard's morning sun. The ticket inspector was sound asleep. It felt like the building's sole remaining purpose was to guard its own impressive silence.

I wandered through a labyrinth of dark stained wood panelled rooms hung with faded 16th century paintings of religious scenes and local dignitaries. The deeper I strayed into the complex the more I wished that I had brought a ball of string to help lead me back out.

The museum described Potosí as 'a small trading post in a desolate patch of the Eastern Andes' before silver was discovered in the Cerro Rico. First christened the Villa Imperial del Carlos V de Potosí on April 1st 1545, some twenty-five thousand miners and tradesmen had moved to the town by 1550. The silver rush was so sudden that it must have seemed as though all roads in the Altiplano led to the boomtown that was blooming out of the desert.

In those early years the population was mainly indigenous, living in circular adobe and straw shelters on or around the lower slopes of the Cerro Rico. At night the fires from thousands of clay ovens would burn like a constellation of angry stars strung across the mountain. These ovens, used to smelt silver from ore, cast a thick pall of smoke that choked the air and blackened the land, preventing any crops from being grown for miles around.

By the end of the 16th century Potosí had matured into a city of over one hundred and twenty thousand souls, similar in size at the time to London and far larger than Madrid, Rome, Seville or Paris. The indigenous population, now mainly a workforce of drafted labor, was housed in segregated 'Indian' parishes on the outskirts of town. Vast engineering works had been carried out in the 1570s to allow lower grade ore to be processed using mercury and water rather than the clay fires of old. A system of thirty two artificial lakes, eighteen dams and hundreds of watermills to power this new refining process ensured the constant supply of silver to the Spanish crown.

Philip II of Spain was as spellbound by the meteoric rise of this precocious city and its priceless mountain as the rest of Europe. He gifted Potosí a shield inscribed with the words: 'For a powerful emperor or a wise king this lofty mountain of silver could conquer the whole world.' Potosí had come to symbolize the fortune, wonder and sheer spectacle of the New World.

I left the Mint to find Plaza 10 de Noviembre in a frenzy of wild celebrations. The local football team, Real Potosí, has beaten Santa Cruz to reach the grand final of the national league. They had returned from the stadium like triumphant war heroes in an open topped bus festooned with balloons and streamers. The whole town had turned out to greet them and I could barely thread my way through the ecstatic crowd. Taxi drivers hooted their horns and threw bangers out of their windows. A couple of brawling drunks had to be herded out of the bus's path.

It was here, in the tight matrix of orderly streets around the central square, that the Spanish owners of the Cerro Rico's four thousand mines squandered their riches with lavish parties and imported luxuries.

Residents marked the coronation of Philip II in 1556 with 24 days of non-stop festivities. There were street processions, bullfights and great banquets held by the wealthy Spanish families. Once finished the richest families are said to have thrown their entire silver dinner services off their balconies to be picked up by passers-by. I wonder if the little dessert spoon that I had bought from the old woman, now buried deep in my pocket, had been tossed from one of these tables.

By the early 17th century the demand for luxury goods from Potosí's status hungry *nouveau riche* was stimulating trade as far afield as China, Panama, Britain and India. Their homes were cluttered with all manner of exotic finery; Persian textiles, Ceylon pearls, porcelain vases, ivory fans, silver jewelry studded with diamonds and fine clothes made from silk and lace. In the evenings they paraded in their finery around the central plaza like royalty, seemingly oblivious to their Andean isolation.

Much of the city's wealth was also poured into the thirty-six magnificent churches that had been completed by the beginning of the 17th century. The local silversmiths, engravers, cabinet makers and painters commissioned to model these churches blended their own native Andean imagery with conventional biblical references to create a unique 'mestizo-baroque' vision of heaven and earth.

The best example of this work is in the stone carved portal of the Iglesia de San Lorenzo de Carangas next to the central market where I had lunch. Here I saw the Christian cross compete with symbols of the sun, moon and stars, a sacred trinity in the Andean world. Vines with ears of corn entwined themselves up the supporting column together with the *Kantuta*, the sacred flower of Incas.

For all of its many churches Potosí never did earn a reputation for piety. By the early 17th century the city also had just as many gambling houses, regularly attended by a loyal congregation of over eight hundred professional gamblers. At night the town's fourteen dance halls swelled with miners. Many, separated from their families and eager to obliterate their experience of life down the mines, blew their wages on *chicha* (a locally brewed maize beer) and women.

At least 120 prostitutes are known to have been working in the city during this period, prompting the Royal Judge Matianzo to complain that 'there is never a shortage of novelty, scandal and wantonness' in Potosí.

When the silver production from the Cerro Rico finally went into decline in the mid 17th century the ministers declared from their pulpits that it was God's revenge on the miners for their wickedness. But no amount of penance could confound the fundamental laws of nature. The earth's natural resources are finite and even the Cerro Rico's seemingly inexhaustible supply of silver was being depleted. By the last quarter of the 17th century modern day Mexico had overtaken Bolivia as the primary silver producer in the New World. Potosí was no longer at the centre of Spain's global ambitions.

Demographic collapse mirrored the city's economic fortunes. Between 1650 and 1700 the population halved from an all time high of one hundred and sixty thousand to seventy three thousand. More and more indigenous workers dodged forced labor and even paid work lost its appeal as the quality of the ore diminished. Wages dipped, shops closed, the markets shrunk and more and more ex-miners begged for alms on the streets. Although there were economic revivals they were short-lived and never matched Potosí's glory days. By the time Bolivia won its independence in 1825, the city had been reduced to a scant nine thousand residents.

Potosí's place in world history has long since shrunk to a couple of page references in the indexes of history books. Potosi, once 'the envy of kings,' has returned to its natural setting – a windblown city in a high flung corner of the world.

I returned to the Hostel Carlos V to find Doña Marta in a terrible mood. She had lost her keys and had no way of leaving without locking herself out of house and home. 'I am fed up with this city you know, it is too cold and business is awful,' she told me in the drafty entrance hall. 'I want to go and live with my cousin in Madrid.'

She talked about Europe as though it was a land of milk and honey and I didn't have the heart to dispel the myth. I guessed that Doña Marta's life was too entwined with Potosi's fate to ever escape its web of distant dreams.

CERRO RICO

In 1598 an old man sees out his remaining days on this earth at the dog end of a tumultuous century. Wracked with fever and covered with seeping sores, Philip II of Spain has been unable to move from his bed for over a month. He is suffering from the last stages of the 'illness of kings,' acute gout. His doctors have told him that there is no hope left other than the miraculous healing powers of prayer, holy water and the touching of his swellings with religious relics.

Left alone in his bedroom for long periods, Philip's only distractions are the echo of footsteps in the long corridor outside, or the whisper of his attendants at the door. El Escorial, his cavernous palace built near Madrid to strict classical proportions, already feels more like a mausoleum than a royal residence.

The days pass slowly. Every dawn he watches a pitiless Castilian sun stretch across the hills of the Sierra de Guadarrama. Every dusk he observes the same hills fold abruptly back into night. In between Philip fitfully traces the course of his forty-two year reign as king and worries about the legacy that his young son is about to inherit.

On paper he is the most powerful man on the planet, the first sovereign to hold sway over the entire Iberian

Peninsula. His European possessions include Naples and Sicily in Southern Europe and the ancient provinces of Flanders and Artois to the North. Beyond the Atlantic, Philip's rule extends over some twenty million square kilometres of land, the vast territories of Latin America.

The reality was that Philip's Spanish empire was beset by a rising tide of revolt and heresy. Protestantism had spread like wild fire across Europe, consuming the Spanish Netherlands in bitter warfare for the previous thirty years. Two disastrous interventions in the French wars of religion had failed to stop a protestant king, Henry of Navarre, ascend to the throne. A pre-emptive naval strike on protestant England had seen the Armada scattered by storm ten years earlier.

Philip's relentless military defence of the empire and the Catholic faith had left the crown bankrupt, forcing humiliating peace treaties with the Dutch and the French. His son Philip III would inherit an impoverished country, exhausted by more than half a century of relentless war and stalked by the spectres of plague and harvest failure. The supreme confidence and burning ambition of the Spanish conquistadors had been replaced by a pervading sense of disillusionment and defeat.

Philip's imperial ambitions had been fuelled by the seemingly inexhaustible flow of silver from the New World. Every Autumn a convoy of Spanish galleons, often more than one hundred strong, would sail into Cádiz laden with tons of silver from the Indies. This massive annual cash injection made Philip's impossible dream of a counter reformation that would unite the world under his sole authority seem possible. But its glittering promise only drew him and his empire into a whirlwind of conflict, debt and ruin.

Most of this silver flowed from the city of Potosí. Is it here that Philip's fevered imagination takes him in his last days and hours? To Potosí, 'the envy of kings,' overlooked by the mountain laced through with silver that they call the Cerro Rico. Does he see the 'Rich Hill' in these final visions, a blessing from the heavens to help carry out God's work on earth? Or does he see another side to the Cerro Rico, the side that has consumed countless souls in his name and pinned his fortunes to a rich but ultimately bitter harvest.

As Philip slipped away at first light on the morning of Sunday 13th of September, the first mass of the day was being sung in the chapel of the Escorial below. Did he, in those final moments, wait on the angels to come down and transport him back up to heaven? Or was it the Cerro Rico's long shadow that he feared, streaking over the Atlantic to fall across his darkening heart.

The slip of yellow paper with a dotted line running along the bottom made for uncomfortable reading. I could be gassed by arsenic, suffocated slowly by a cave-in, ripped to shreds in an explosion or exposed to lung choking dust leading to silicosis. There was space below for me to fill in my passport number and next of kin in case someone needed to be informed of my abrupt end. I signed on the dotted line, waiving any responsibility by the tour company should anything go wrong on my journey down the mines of the Cerro Rico.

'Don't worry, we haven't had an accident in twenty years,' the ex-miner behind the desk assured me with a wink from his one remaining eye.

Gringo tours down the Cerro Rico have become an essential source of alternative income for many ex-miners. Agencies have sprung up all around the central plaza, each desperate to attract the same passing trade. A life-sized mannequin of a tall, blond youth dressed in ill-fitting protective clothing and a hard hat leaned precariously out of one agency's front door. Another office was plastered with pictures of an old truck with a large yellow hard hat perched on top of it. A group of *gringos* sat on the bonnet and grinned beneath a speech bubble that read: 'We got the miner's truck.'

I chose the least flashy, longest standing company but was already feeling uneasy about my tour the following day. It wasn't any real or imagined risk to life and limb that worried me. It was the way the trip was packaged up as a cross between a high adrenaline sport and a safari.

'Step right up,' I imagined the ticket touts calling out at the entrance to the mine, 'join the ultimate in extreme mining, the death tour of the Cerro Rico.'

Although tourists have being going down these mines since the early 1980s, in recent years the experience has become far more prescribed. When I first visited Potosí the independent miners would approach travellers arriving from La Paz on the night bus at dawn. I remember one of these miners taking me down to where he was working a deep vein of tin with his teenage son. We descended through a series of holes and tunnels barely the width of a man. I didn't have any protective clothing and was warned of the deadly gases that occasionally crept through the area we were in from disused shafts that date back to the Spanish colonial era. The miners kept a constant eye on the naked flame from their calcium carbonate lamp. Any change in color or intensity warned them of the silent advance of an invisible killer.

By the time we made it back to the light of day I felt as if the miner and his son were friends as well as guides. We had shared something of our life stories and made a connection between cultures, oceans and huge economic inequalities. The money and presents of *coca* and alcohol that I gave went straight to their family, it seemed a fairer exchange than today's more organised tours.

The experience this time round was safer, more formalized and far more intense. By eight-thirty the following morning I found myself standing in a long line of some thirty tourists being inspected by guides. It felt like our first day in the army. They ordered us to strip down to jeans and a T-shirt and size us up for protective clothing. Standard combat fatigues were wellington boots, a matching grey overcoat and over-trousers, a hard hat and a head torch with a large battery pack slung around the waist.

Our guides kept up a constant banter in broken English while we bickered over who was going to have the last pair of size forty-four wellies.

'You Scottish, yes Sean Connery, turn off your head lamp. You model girl, give me your shoes.' The youngest and cockiest of the guides gathered up all of our shoes into his arms and did a Charlie Chaplin stagger into the storeroom before collapsing with them all into a heap. It was a well-worn routine.

We were quickly divided into groups and introduced to our 'personal' guide Rolando. My platoon was made up of a young Canadian couple, an American girl, a stout Italian man in his early fifties, a German lad and two terrified looking Swiss girls. Rolando was an ex-miner in his late thirties with a red bandana tied around his neck and a slow, laconic lilt. He reminded me of the cowboys in 1950s Westerns that squinted into the middle distance for a living. He give us a long tired look, spat into the sand and said: 'It is time to go to the mountain.'

Our first stop was the busy Plaza Calvario on the outskirts of town to buy soft drinks, coca, cigarettes and dynamite as gifts for the miners that we would come across on our underground tour. The street market, supplying the miners of Cerro Rico, is open day and night and hums with an air of urgency and exhaustion. The visiting miners were either winding up for work or winding down with a few refreshments having just knocked off from a gruelling twelve-hour shift.

Plaza Calvario was a shadow of the frenzied mood that must have infected Potosi in its colonial heyday. The entire town's centre was once dominated by a sprawling open market that matched the Cerro Rico for sheer spectacle. In a society of strict racial segregation this was the one space where Spaniards, Quechua, Aymara and African slaves would have rubbed shoulders in a feverish atmosphere of commerce and gossip.

Called *Galo del Gato*, a Spanish adaptation from Quechua meaning the 'Market of Indian Ladies,' the street stalls were packed with solid fuel, food, silver and coca. Most important of all was the coca. One 16th century Potosí resident, Luis Capoche, described seeing endless baskets piled high with coca leaves, 'placed at the doors where many Indian women trade it for ore or silver.'

These Quechua and Aymara tradeswomen were part of a new economic and social force in colonial upper Peru. Freed from their bonds of service to the crown or their home communities many of these tradeswomen, known as *Yanaconas*, grew independently wealthy. The

Yanaconas spoke a smattering of Spanish, dressed in finely woven native textiles known as *cumbi*, and wore high hats with wide brims typical of the area. Their descendents are today's *cholas*, with their pleated skirts and bowler hats, who continue to sell their produce in the Altiplano's markets with the same mix of charm and hard-nosed commercial nous.

The little adobe building that we ducked into with Rolando was stacked with fizzy liquids to combat dehydration, raw cane alcohol for blessings, and dynamite for blasting. Rolando was particularly keen to introduce us to the pyrotechnics. He unrolled the wrapping paper from a stick of dynamite as we stood in a small circle in the confined shop and insisted we pass it around. The smooth green stick of nitro-glycerine looked and felt as innocent as Brighton rock, only chewier, like hardened bubblegum.

Rolando attached a long slow fuse with a metal conductor, held a lighter next to it and told us that 'this is the preferred toy of Bolivian miners, street protestors, road blocks and revolutionary acts of terror.'

There was a stunned silence, eventually broken by the German who grinned nervously and asks if he could blow something up.

Rolando, relishing his role more than ever, nodded slowly and said 'yes my friend, we will try this out later.'

As our bus wound up a dirt road towards the Cerro Rico, Potosí dropped away beneath us. The tin roofs of the miners' homes on the outskirts caught a fearsome reflection from an unblinking sun. Communities such as this once fought hard to usher in a new era of labour reform with the overthrow of old mining interests in 1952. A new state mining company called the *Corporación Minera de Bolivia* (Comibol) took over two thirds of the country's private mines, totalling a workforce of twenty thousand men. Wages and working conditions improved for Comibol miners until a combination of inefficiency and falling mineral prices forced its closure in the late 1980s.

Despite Comibol's demise several thousand miners continue to work the deep seams of the Cerro Rico for its remaining deposits of silver, zinc, iron, tin and lead. The vast majority of these workers belong to one of around thirty mining cooperatives. Mining in cooperatives may sound like the marketing blurb on a Fair Trade label but the reality is that there is no capital to invest in equipment, healthcare, safety, or pensions. Miners scratch a miserable living in conditions reminiscent of the old colonial days of silver mining in the Cerro Rico.

From a distance the hill itself looked deserted, its red earth long stripped of any vegetation. But as we got closer I realized that there were men working all over the surface like black termites. I had heard that the Cerro Rico is so riddled with tunnels that it has dropped several metres in height and is so hollow that the entire hill is in danger of sudden collapse.

In my mind's eye I saw the mountain one day being flattened completely in a controlled explosion, like a condemned high-rise block of flats. Would the town's residents line up and cheer, or would they mourn the loss of such a reliable source of deadly employment?

'You know that as many as nine million miners have perished in the Cerro Rico, most of them during Spanish colonial rule,' Rolando shouted over the straining engine of our ancient bus.

Nine million. The sheer scale of the figure is staggering, so hard to take in. I rolled it around in my mind and tried to imagine the hundreds of thousands of miners who would have trudged up this hill every dawn during the colonial period, leading llamas laden with tools, candles and coca. Rolando told us that if twenty healthy workers entered the colonial mines of the Cerro Rico on Monday for a week's work, only half would hobble back out alive by the following Saturday.

News of the suffering of these mainly Quechua workers from the surrounding regions did filter back to Europe. As early as 1550 the Dominican monk Domingo de Santo Tomás complained that the Potosí mine owners treated their labourers like wild dogs. He compared the Cerro Rico to the mouth of hell into which 'a great mass of people enter every year and are sacrificed by the greed of the Spaniards to their God.'

An intense but ultimately inconclusive moral debate over the fate of the 'Indians' raged within the Catholic Church. Even Philip II, so dependant on silver to fund his foreign ventures, was shaken by the treatment of his subjects in the New World.

In 1564 he wrote to the Archbishop of Lima, concerned that 'many Indians hang themselves...others take poisoned herbs, mothers kill their babies saying they do it to free them from the hardships they themselves suffer.'

But no amount of hand wringing and royal proclamations affording Indians and Spaniards the same rights could make up for the crown's insatiable desire for silver. The abuses of the forced labour or '*mita*' system continued unreformed until the lands around the Cerro Rico were emptied of its people. By the middle of the 17th century three quarters of the surrounding population had been wiped out.

Back in La Paz I had recently seen a documentary about the Chernobyl disaster with grainy footage of men being bused into the disaster zone in flimsy mackintoshes to protect them from the lethal radiation. Suddenly it felt as though I have become part of this footage, bumping down a road on a vintage bus in our protective gear towards a site of similar horror.

A pale dust had settled, layer upon layer, on everything at the entrance of the mine. The dust sat on the low buildings, the upturned iron carriage for transporting ore, the small gauge railway track. The normally red earth looked like it has been covered with a fine spindrift of snow. It felt like walking straight into a black and white negative with the lights and darks inverted.

The sole miner at the entrance to the tunnel looked like an apparition. His body was white from the dust, his eyes red from exhaustion. His name was Lucas and at just twenty years of age he had already been working in this section of the mine for four years.

He had just completed a fourteen hour shift, working through the night on a vein that had held out much promise but had failed to come good. 'It is mostly rubbish down there,' he told me, 'the price of silver is very good right now but most of it has long been taken.'

These days silver only makes up around 2% of the ore extracted from the Cerro Rico. Lucas told me with boundless optimism that one day he would stumble on a hidden vein of rock laced with riches. But he was also well aware of the dangers.

'I have to make my money while I am young,' he told me. 'Two of my uncles have black lung and can't work anymore'.

Black lung is the local term for silicosis, a scarring and inflammation of the lungs caused by years of inhaling the fine dust that had settled around us. It is largely responsible for cutting the miner's life expectancy to a mere 40 years old.

No wonder Lucas was already considering early retirement. 'Once I have the money to buy a car I am going to give this up and become a taxi driver,' he admitted.

I gave Lucas the stick of dynamite that Rolando had been passing around earlier. 'Thanks, I'll need this to kill the mother-in-law,' he quipped as I returned to my group.

We left Lucas at the entrance and plunged into a long tunnel that quickly muffled out any sound apart from our breath, our footsteps and the constant hiss from an overhead plastic pipe transporting oxygen to shafts deeper in the mine. For the first hundred yards we walked erect under high catacombs of interwoven stone, which seemed more like the nave of a cathedral than a mineshaft. Rolando explained that this was the original Spanish gallery, constructed in the 16th century when they had the materials and manpower to invest.

We pushed on into the more recent shafts on our hands and knees, scrambling through uneven worm holes with odd bits of wood for support over narrow walkways across cavernous drops. My vision shrank to the rear end of the sluggish Italian in front of me, fixed in the narrow shaft of light from my head torch.

Dust rose and fell across the beam like fine silt in an underwater documentary and I half expected to see the bow of a sunken ship appear out of the gloom ahead of me. The only too real sighting was the Italian's bum cleavage, which rose up like a shipwreck's ghostly prow every time he went into a crawl.

Eventually we reached a low alcove where the shaft petered out into a dead end. We squatted on two makeshift wooden benches and tried to catch our breath. The altitude, exertion and rising heat were already taking its toll. I avoided any eye contact that might give away my fear and looked to Rolando now as the only man who could lead us out of this hell alive.

'The deeper you delve into this dormant volcano the hotter it gets,' Rolando told us, as if we hadn't already noticed. The temperature peaks in some shafts of Cerro Rico are at the limits of human tolerance, around forty-five Celsius.

As our eyes adjusted to our surroundings I suddenly noticed an addition to our group. At the end of the low alcove a hunched figure held court over our disorientated party. He had coal black eyes, a gaping mouth, two horns curling out of the top of his head and a bright red erection. His body was covered with desiccated coca leaves and empty plastic bottles of alcohol. Cigarette ends were littered around his feet and a flickering candle chased shadows across his waxy face. 'This is the miner's devil, known as *El Tío*, the owner of the underworld,' Rolando explained. "If you see *El Tío*, the devil, walking around, you can go crazy or die of fear. *El Tío* is God here: if he wants accidents, he will have them.'

Representations of *El Tío* are tucked into the corners of makeshift shrines throughout the mountain. The miners continuously offer up pure cane alcohol, cigarettes and coca leaves to ask for future prosperity and to calm his notorious temper. On key dates in their religious calendar the miners also sacrifice llamas at the entrance to the mines in the hope that *El Tío*'s blood lust will be sated by the llama blood that they spray over the rocks.

El Tío is thought to have originated with an old Incan belief in a more benign earth spirit that protected miners who strayed into his domain. Under the Spanish the belief was suppressed as a pagan aberration. But this spirit was not for taming. The devil in the mountain returned to haunt the miners' imagination soon after Bolivian independence. Only this time, perhaps informed by the experience of colonial rule, this God of the underworld had taken on a vicious streak. Now he is both protector and executioner and is often characterised with curly hair and a pointed beard, the stylized features of a Spanish conquistador.

El Tío has come to personify a world where uncertainty and death are as ever present as the mine's darkness. He is their silent arbitrator, doling out wealth, illness and suffering with total indifference. Any accident in the mine is quickly attributed to *El Tío's* violent temper, any good fortune evidence of his generosity.

I stared at this monstrous creation of papier-maché and poster paint and realised that *el Tío* was as real to me as to the miners that created him. My devil in the mountain is my father, a fantastical figure who loomed over the hinterland of my imagination with wild eyes and the invested power of my creation.

Rolando's voice drifted back to me. He was telling us how women are normally excluded from the mine. '*El Tío* and the Earth goddess *Pachamama* are partners and together they seed the mountain with its minerals,' he was saying. 'If women enter the mine *El Tío* will want to possess them and the *Pachamama* will become jealous. They will fight and the mountain's fertility will drop.' He assured us that the women in our group were allowed to visit because they wore long trousers rather than the traditional *pollera* or skirt, which was too much temptation for *El Tío's* inflamed passions.

Rolando scattered an offering of a handful of coca leaves around the figure of *El Tío* as he mapped out the next couple of hours of light entertainment. 'We will descend down through three different levels of the mine and each new level will be hotter and further from the earth's surface,' he told us. 'The old state mine had sixteen levels' Rolando continued, 'but the pumps failed when it closed and the bottom eight have been flooded with water ever since. They now lie under the water table, below the level of Potosí.'

Images from the cavernous halls of Milton's *Paradise Lost* filled my mind. Staring into the hollow eyes of *El Tío's* monstrous indifference I felt the heat, oppression and madness of the Cerro Rico's cold heart rising up to overtake me. I desperately tried to focus on the thin battery lights dim illumination and the sharp intake of each new breath. But I could barely suppress the wave of terror that was rising inside me. It felt like I was falling into the pitch darkness that pushed in around us – a blackness so complete that it could extinguish my soul, like so many others before it, in an instant.

I screwed up my eyes and dug my nails into the palms of my hands. Stinging pain and a single image came to my rescue. It was of a kite, a huge blue kite with a long spiraling trail flying high in a powder blue sky. I was nestled back in my father's arms and he was holding me and the kite steady, his hands clenched in tight fists around handles attached to two taught lines of string. The lines dipped and shimmered and disappeared and reappeared on their long, arcing journey up to my kite, a tiny and defiant arrow edging into the wind.

We were by the sea near Glenelg in Scotland and I must have been about nine years old. My father had bought the stunt kite for my birthday. When we first took it out of the packaging it seemed huge, a bundle of plastic sheeting and wooden dowel struts. He said it was the only kite he could find that was strong enough to handle the West Coast winds. When we first tried to launch the hulking superstructure it lumbered off the ground for a moment before quickly succumbing to gravity. My dad told me not to lose heart, my 1970s 'sports stunt kite' just needed a gale to fly in.

We didn't have to wait long. A keen and steady easterly struck up a few days later and we took the kite with a great sense of ceremony to the marshy brown flats past the red phone box at the end of the village. The sea was just beyond, running fast between the mainland and the township of Kylerhea on Skye. We stopped short of the beach, far enough away to prevent a watery crash landing. It was the perfect day for our kite's maiden voyage – bright and sunny but with a constant wind that cut though our clothes and doubled us over in the gusts. I remember Dad in his brown flares, flapping wildly in the wind.

We laid the kite flat on the ground and walked backwards, uncoiling line from the handles like two sappers laying explosives in a Second World War movie. At 20 metres we stopped and I walked back to launch the kite, while dad held the lines tight. This time it immediately felt prone and alive when I held it up into the wind. 'One, two, three launch!' shouted my father and I hurled the beast with its long, red tickertape tail into the sky. It rocketed up into the sky, performed a violent 180 turn and kamikazeed straight back at me. Diving to the ground it buried its nose in a peat bog next to me.

After several more failed attempts the kite finally took wing, its battle weary sails now slapping loosely against the cross bar as it juddered up and up into what seemed to me like the outer stratosphere. My Dad had to shout instructions to me as the wind picked up and we both squinted into the sun to keep sight of the speck of deep blue drawing red lines across an open canvas. Kneeling down he told me to stand between his arms. One by one I took the handles and felt the almost irresistible pull on the line, like some enormous fish that hasn't yet broken the surface.

Dad showed me how to make an O in the sky, how to then steady the kite and loop the other way to keep the lines clear of each other. With every turn I felt the kite grow stronger, more confident. Its clean lines still dip and rise in my mind, my father and I never more united in direction, or purpose.

Somewhere far below we heard the rasp of shovels as miners loaded up another bucket of rocks to be transported to the surface. The man in front of us was turning a hand winch, hauling the ore, bucket by bucket, up to our level. Rolando handed him a bottle of fizzy drink and some coca as an incentive to stop this work for long enough to let us clamber down the same shaft. We slid bit by bit down the tunnel sideways, pushing our legs and arms against the sides to avoid careering into the miners below.

We dropped one by one into a large chamber with three miners excavating a pit of rubble from a recent blast of dynamite. Two of the men were breaking up rocks with picks and shovels while the third filled up the buckets from a wheelbarrow to be hoisted back up the shaft that we had just clambered down. They were stripped down to their trousers, their bodies gleaming with sweat in our torch light, their faces contorted by a *bola* of coca leaves in one cheek.

We sat around the high edge of the rubble and watched the men work together, the rhythm and monotony of their labor dulling their pain and exhaustion. They appeared to be in a trance, somnambulic beings from the underworld tearing away at the mountain's insides with their bare hands. They could be from any era, their methods largely unchanged since the first shaft was sunk into the Cerro Rico's side in the 16th Century.

It was as though the veil of time had lifted. This little scene was a view across five hundred years of mining in the Cerro Rico. It was also a single frame from the engine house of ruin for millions of souls. I swear I could hear phrases of Quechua and the scrape of tools down long abandoned shafts all around us. I realized that despite its many aliases the Cerro Rico has only one true name: 'The mountain that eats men'.

'Is anyone going to come down here and give us a hand?' one of the miners asked. I was jarred back to the group and suddenly felt ashamed to be part of this lurid voyeurism. We were perched around the miners like carrion, hungrily feeding our curiosity for the macabre. Sure we would pay them off with some sugared drinks and a couple of sticks of dynamite, but then zoo animals get biscuits for their troubles too.

When Rolando indicated that it was time to head back out of the mine the collective sense of relief was palpable. Step by step we cautiously negotiated the steep climb through a warren of shafts before finally emerging to a harsh afternoon light. We must have looked like dusty wraiths to the next round of fresh-faced tourists queuing up to take our place in the mountain's antechambers somewhere far behind us. No one spoke much afterwards, but shock at the inhumanity of the Cerro Rico, or perhaps just fate itself, was reflected in everyone's eyes.

The cocky German lad who wanted to blow things up got his firework display in the end. Rolando lit the long fuse on a stick of dynamite and insisted on posing for photos with his arms around the ladies and the lit nitroglycerine lodged between his teeth. He then sauntered with a bow legged gait into waste ground to lay the charge in loose soil. The explosion rocked the earth and smoke curled high into the air, rippling a shock wave through us all.

The rumbling report of the dynamite seemed a fitting note to end my visit to the Cerro Rico. The name Potosí is said to come from *potojsi*, Quechua for thunder. It was the sound of a voice that was said to emit from deep within the mountain when the eleventh Incan king Huayna Capac considered surveying the Cerro Rico for minerals, years before the arrival of the Spanish. 'This is not for you' the voice said, 'God is keeping these riches for those that come from afar.' Huayna Capac, the last undisputed king of the Incas, left the mountain's harvest untouched for his successors.

SUCRE

There was no marker point for Tarapaya on the road between Potosi and Sucre. The driver just stopped the bus and pointed vaguely beyond a scree of rough ground on the other side of a dry riverbed. 'Watch yourself' he warned tapping his index finger just below his eye, 'the spring is bewitched.'

I climbed slowly up the track that led out of the far side of the riverbed, through dry brush and loose stone. The ragged peaks of the surrounding *Cordillerra Occidental* seemed to have been speared to the sky by the midday sun. 'The light like glass at 2pm,' I remembered an English expatriate saying when I asked what she loved most about the Altiplano.

Before long the sound of running water broke the spell of silence and sunlight and I crossed a stream of bubbling grey water. Up ahead a small group of men and women dressed in black were dipping their faces in the water. They stopped to stare at me as I walked past. Beyond them lay the hot spring of Tarapaya.

It looked like the sort of mirage a desperate man lost in some nameless desert would catch sight of. A wide ellipse of water surrounded by lush green grasses jumped out from the desiccated yellow, ochre and russet of the parched landscape. On one side of the spring there were two low white buildings. The valley dropped away sharply beyond the shimmering water, opening into a wide panorama of mountains and sky.

The view must have been unchanged since Huayna Capac reputedly stood in the same spot in the early 16th century, only a few years before the *conquistadores* arrived. Tarapaya was once a favoured spot for Incan royalty who trekked for weeks across the Andes from Cusco to bathe in its sacred waters. When Huayna Capac visited this southern edge of the Incan province of Collasuyu he was the undisputed master of a vast empire, stretching some three thousand miles north into modern day Colombia.

I stood at the edge of the spring and stared into its opaque depths, a clouded mirror masking serpentine currents beneath. These waters would unsettle anyone. Perhaps even Huayna Capac had a sense of his own mortality here. I wondered if he contemplated the prediction that his death would herald the collapse of the Incan empire. The Incas believed that their God Viracocha would vengefully return from the sea in the 12th Incan dynasty with his robe trailing a long wake behind him.

'It is bottomless,' a voice said behind me. I turned to see a small man standing at my heels wearing a fisherman's sleeveless jacket full of stuffed pockets and a deerstalker on his head. The skin on his face had been cured by the sun like beef jerky. 'I am the warden,' he told me. 'Swim with care, you can only stand at the very edge and there is a current in the centre that pulls people under.' He pointed at the group I had just passed and added, 'that's the grieving family of the last person who drowned here, he was drunk. I never find their bodies you know.'

After charging me a nominal 'entry fee' the warden resumed his long vigil on a small bench on the far side of the water. I was his only visitor and wondered at this man's lifeguard skills if I did get into trouble in the current. His fishing jacket, bulging with mysterious equipment, would sink him long before he could ever reach me. It occurred to me, with a twinge of panic, that this fellow had more to say about the disappearing swimmers than he was letting on.

I stripped off regardless and edged into the spring's muddy shallows. It felt like swimming in a bowl of hot, green milk. I could barely see my own arms under the surface and imagined the drowned dancing slow tangos in capricious currents somewhere beneath me. The occasional gas bubble broke the surface, a sulphurous belch from the bowels of the earth.

As I swam cautiously around the spring's wide circumference it felt as though I was being watched by many more eyes than the wardens. I wondered if this place was indeed bewitched. The locals call this spring '*el ojo del Inca*,' the eye of the Inca. Perhaps this is the portal through which the Inca kings continue to observe proceedings in their old kingdoms, much as the Greek Gods spied on their mortal champions in Homer's epic narratives.

The Incan rulers are certainly revered more in death than in life. Huayna Capac's corpse was embalmed and worshipped long after his empire had crumbled. The Spanish found his mummified body some twenty-five years after he had died, wrapped in fine textiles with only the tip of his nose missing.

Huayna Capac would have heard reports of the white man's arrival but he never lived to meet them. He was struck down, along with his heir Ninan Cuyochi, by a terrible fever while garrisoned with his army at Timipampa near Quito in Ecuador, sometime between 1525 and 1527. The mystery illness, which is said to have wiped out thousands, may well have been a smallpox epidemic. It was the first of several deadly European viruses to devastate the native population who had no defenses to these alien diseases.

Had Huayna Capac survived he would have easily crushed the Spanish *conquistadores* that first landed in Incan territory on the coast of Peru in 1532. Francisco Pizarro's rag tag company of only 180 men and 37 horses was no match for the imperial Incan forces that ran into tens of thousands of disciplined warriors. As it was, they set foot in an empire torn apart by bitter civil war between Huayna Capac's surviving sons Huayna and Atahualpa and ripe for the taking. Within a year of arriving Huayna and Atahualpa were both dead and Spain's astonishing victory in the New World complete.

Pizarro caught up with Atahualpa, fresh from victory over his brother, at the shores of the hot springs of Calamarca on the 25th of September 1532. On a tour of his northern territories Atahualpa commanded an army of an estimated 80,000 men. Pizarro's men were impressed, one of them describing the army at night as *"a fearful sight, they were camped on a hillside and so close to one another that it looked like a brilliant star-studded sky."*

It seems that for all of Atahualpa's military superiority he fatefully underestimated the Spaniard's ruthless ambition and lust for gold. Lured into a meeting with his men unarmed, the conquistadores fell on them with swords and cannon grapeshot. Some 7,000 were massacred in the bloodbath that followed at Calamarca and Atahualpa was captured.

Within a couple of hours Pizarro had acquired an empire. Atahualpa's army was impotent without their supreme leader who was worshipped as a deity. The mortal man bargained for his freedom, promising to fill a room with gold and silver in return for his release. His throne weighed 183 pounds of solid gold alone and over the following months an estimated 24 tons of silver and 11 tons of gold artifacts were fed to the Spanish furnaces. But the king's ransom wasn't enough. In a hastily convened trial Atahualpa was convicted of treason for 'incestuous polygamy and worshiping false gods.' He was garroted before being burnt at the stake on the 26th of July, 1533. Before he died the friar Valverde swapped his sword for a cross, baptizing the hapless Atahualpa 'Francisco' and instructing him in the good tenants of the Christian faith.

'*Buena onda*' I heard someone say as I reached the bank. A tall, lean man in his mid 20s with long black hair stood waiting on the edge. He sported a loose fitting sleeveless t-shirt over a muscular body and pair of baggy shorts. His hands were busy, intently sanding something the size of a large pebble. The phrase *buena onda* alone, which means good vibes, immediately identified him as an '*artisano*'.

The *artisanos* are South America's modern day hippies. Drifting across borders with a bag of hand made jewelry and a set of idle dreams they live for freedom, good times and more often than not a line of coke. It is the cheap living that draws so many of them to Bolivia. Most come from Argentina and Chile, middle class kids following in Che Guevara's footsteps, selling bracelets for a couple of years before returning to their relatively comfortable lives.

I don't know why I have always been so cynical about these artisans. Perhaps it's jealousy. The guys ooze Latin charm with their hypnotic eyes, raven hair and Cuban protest songs strummed out on a broken guitar. They can seduce any unsuspecting *gringa* from a thousand yards. Next to them I felt like the archetypal Brit out in the midday sun.

'I am making this with wood from an ancient forest that we cycled through on the border with Argentina,' the young man told me. He held out his hand to reveal a sun medallion, fashioned out of a dark grainy wood and curved snugly into the palm of his hand. Some of my frostiness melted. It was a beautiful little object that told of hours of patient craftsmanship.

Antonio showed me a shawl covered with his work. There were bracelets of tightly woven green lizards, necklaces of rows of men chasing each other with spears, shark's teeth and leather pendants. I marvelled at the workmanship as he told me how he drew his inspiration from indigenous cultures and cave paintings he had seen on his travels.

We sat on the steps of one of the little white houses and drank *mate* from a gourd with a metal straw while he spun tales of his travels by bicycle with his girlfriend. They had cycled all the way from Mendoza in Argentina and were headed for Lake Titicaca. They gathered materials along the way, mainly stones, reeds, wood and seeds to make and sell jewelry to pay for their travels. They lived on fruit and *mate*, stopping at places like Tarapaya for long periods of gentle industry. Each piece of jewelry was several days in the making.

I was impressed. With all this talk of climate change and global footprints here were a couple who were quietly leading by example. They made no demands on the earth they cycled over, turning little offerings from the natural world into glittering sparks of human imagination. 'When we run out of fruit, *mate* and bottled water I cycle into Potosi and sell a few pieces of jewelry to fund the next week or so. We never go hungry,' Antonio told me.

They seemed genuinely at peace with themselves and content to witness each day's gradual passing. 'We have no distractions,' Antonio explains. 'Out here there is only the sun's slow arc across the sky for entertainment – I spend most of my day listening to the silence.'

I sat down by the spring's edge to take stock. The contrast between this couple's Zen-like meander through Bolivia and my half crazed stampede couldn't have been more marked. I was cluttering my days with experiences in the hope that they would bring me closer to the region, its people and ultimately my father along the way. And yet in all this frenetic activity I had not stopped once, until now, to listen.

In the Altiplano the silence is almost audible. It hangs expectant, like the pause after a question. It felt as though a vast velvet bell had been rung out there in the shimmering Andes. In the stillness I turned over memories of my father from my childhood like precious stones. They are so fractured, incomplete.

The clearest are of long days spent outdoors. Like being carried high on his shoulders through snow in the Blue Mountains of Australia, or building a dam with clods of peaty earth in the burn behind our cottage in Glenelg.

The rest are distant flashes of moments in time: Walking on his feet up and down a long hall; snuggled up to him in a wing-backed chair by the fire in the dead of winter; reading the adventures of *The Little Grey*

Men; watching him from a bedroom window in London walk smartly away down a rain-swept street.

When he was away, my brother and I missed him as though in the grip of a physical addiction. Years later we admitted to each other that we both crept into his closet to bury our heads into the armpits of his shirts, inhaling deep draughts of his scent. I remember standing in his empty shoes, feeling the instep that his feet had worn into the soles, as though seeking physical proof of his existence. As we grew up this somehow defined us, the absence of a presence.

'We'll see each other again on the road,' Antonio shouted after me as I walked back down the hill to catch a lift to Sucre. It crossed my mind that it is Antonio, not the warden, who was the true guardian of the spring of Tarapaya.

The painting of the Virgin of Guadeloupe arrived in the white city of Sucre's central plaza loaded unceremoniously onto the flatbed of a white pickup. The first I saw of it was a wobbly box with a glass front being held upright by two armed police, standing on the back of the gleaming Toyota. The dancers followed on behind – men jumping and spinning in bright blue costumes with silver trim. Finally the band appeared, letting rip a fanfare of brass as the pickup approached the steps of the city's main cathedral.

The procession stopped abruptly, allowing the band to down their instruments and gingerly hoist the Virgin onto a specially constructed viewing platform. Her dress, a wide triangle of gold, silver and sapphire, sparkled spectacularly against the whitewashed cathedral walls.

Painted by a local artist in 1601, the Virgin of Guadeloupe has taken on celebrity status in Sucre,

Bolivia's nominal capital. She is believed to watch protectively over its citizens, granting the wishes of the most pious and deserving. Over the centuries the town's wealthy have adorned her dress with precious gems, in the hope of winning divine favour. Residents joke that the value of the painting's jewels alone could pay off the country's entire foreign debt.

Once the painting had been placed in the colonial square of high palm trees and grand facades everyone bowed their heads in silent prayer – a moment of civil respect to mark the opening of the Festival. As we all stood in repose the distant sound of drums and horns filtered into the square on the cool morning air. Communities from all over the eastern Altiplano had already started dancing the long route to the Virgin from the outskirts of town.

Sucre's citizens seemed well geared up for a weekend of wild revelry. Entire extended families had turned up laden with cushions, fizzy drinks, children's toys and umbrellas to shade out the sun. They packed every spare inch of the streets on the dancers' route into town, renting numbered sections of the curbs for around three dollars a metre. For one day every year this pavement must be the most sought after real estate in town.

A sprawling camp of attendant street vendors had also sprung up, offering the gathering crowds endless rounds of snacks and refreshments. Chorizo sausages, a local delicacy, bubble away in wide pans of black oil. Delicately fashioned balls of potato mash had been fried and neatly stacked in pyramids. There was roast pork, ox tongue and *charque*, cooked up with boiled potatoes, egg and corn.

Most people were drinking *chicha*, a maize drink fermented with human saliva and served in a gourd shaped like a hollow cow's horn. The big *chola* woman who offered me a sample grinned and told me: 'If you don't drink, the Virgin will be offended.' One sip of her *chicha* threw up a long buried memory of the cider that I used to swig from plastic bottles as a teenager. Excessive eating and boozing is an important part of the cycle of religious festivals that regularly punctuate the hardship of life in the Altiplano.

It wasn't long before Sucre's first troops of costumed dancers burst into the central square. I was immediately spellbound by the tall, devilish creatures that bobbed and swayed in the brilliant sunlight. Dressed in blood red robes, they wore leering masks with bulging eyes, twisted horns and tangled hair that seethed with lizards and serpents. There was an air of oppression to their repetitive steps and the bands' monotonous tones, as though they are undergoing an act of penance as well as celebration.

The man sitting next to me kept up a running commentary as the dancers lumbered past. 'That's the *Diablada*,' he told me. 'It tells the story of Archangel Miguel's triumph over the devil.' In truth the *Diablada's* biblical reference masks far deeper, pagan legends. The devilish dancers are also thought to represent the *Supays*, pre-Christian spirits that inhabit the Incan underworld.

Religious festivals in the Altiplano are a vivid reminder that the Spanish may have conquered the New World, but they couldn't wipe out its people's collective memory. Even the fanatical adoration of the Virgin Mary in towns like Sucre harks back to pre-Christian beliefs. The cult of the Virgin has merged with the worship of the Pachamama, the goddess of fertility and abundance that still has a profound influence on the ebb and flow of daily life in the Andes.

The dances gave a bewildering snapshot of Bolivia's different regions and people. A group of young men swung past in a blur of red and yellow dancing the *Tinku* in cow-hide hats fashioned like conquistadors' helmets. An Aymara tradition, the *Tinku* began as a form of ritualised hand-to-hand combat between slaves during the Spanish conquest.

Although celebrated as a national dance its roots are firmly in northern Potosi where a big meeting, or *Tinku,* is held between rival communities every May. In Potosi and especially in the town of Santiago de Macha, these encounters descend into bloody brawls with upwards of 3,000 participants often hurling rocks and using shards of glass to inflict maximum damage to their opponents. Fatalities are common, although any bloodshed is considered a worthy sacrifice to the Pachamama in return of course for fertility and a good harvest.

Next came the Guarani from the arid Chaco region in the extreme southwest of the country. The men danced the *Chacarera*, elegant steps for these gauchos in buttoned up suits and cowboy boots. The women who partnered them reminded me of Andalucían flamenco dancers with their long, flowing dresses and tied back hair.

The *Tobas* dancers who appeared later, representing tribes from the Bolivian Amazon and Oriente, were the most exotic. Rows of warriors with high feathered head pieces and long spears were led by terrifying shamans, covered in furs, ram horns and papier-mâché human skulls. Even in the bright sunlight, their flowing white hair and grimacing masks sent a shiver down my spine.

Watching this procession of diversity file past, it struck me that Bolivia isn't really a nation at all. It is more a loose collection of different ethnic groups, divided by history, vast tracts of rough terrain and a state that can barely hold the centre. I realised that there wasn't a single yellow, green and red flag of the Bolivian republic in the crowd. These communities chose to dance under the *Wiphala* instead, the rainbow of colour that celebrates the country's plurinational identity, made up of 36 different indigenous groups.

By nightfall the casualties were mounting up. Girls with broken heels and blisters sat on the pavements rubbing their toes. Many of the band members were so drunk that the spectators had to keep escorting them back into line. A handful of colourful feathers, an angel's wing and a golden cross lay scattered like discarded trophies for the gods at my feet.

But still they kept coming. Miners from Oruro, practically an ethnic group unto themselves, streamed into the plaza at around midnight (darkness is their domain). Eerie and ghost-like in the glow of their head torches, they ceremoniously bashed the road with their picks, hammers and pneumatic drills.

By two in the morning Sucre's legendary conservatism and reserve finally slipped as exhaustion and alcohol took hold. A group of students showed me how to dance the *Caporales* – a cross-over between salsa and an energetic waltz. It was all going well until, in a moment of high spirits, I swung one of the girls so enthusiastically that she knocked over her bewildered boyfriend.

They moved on quickly, leaving me with Pablo, a forlorn-looking youth dressed in a beige shirt and chaps over black baggy trousers and boots. He gripped me firmly by the arm, more in search of support than friendship, and tapped out a bewildering series of steps that make up the *Chacarera*. What impressed me most was the way his legs moved with such agility, while the rest of his body swayed alarmingly in the non-existent wind.

'I'm a cowboy, like a Texan you know, but I'm from the Chaco,' he mumbled proudly, 'Mustang, they are the best horses, we have Argentinean horses which are good, but Mustang are the toughest.' Having dispensed with the small talk, Pablo settled a firm hand on my shoulder and peered into my eyes as though seeking out treasure in a dark cave. 'Now tell me,' he asked, 'How can I screw Swedish girls – you know what I mean, don't you?' he added, making a series of ever more explicit hand gestures to emphasis his point.

'You know the problem is that my English is no good,' Pablo explained. He told me his one and only chat-up line: 'Hello, I love you.' I tried to point out that Swedish girls probably need a lot more polite chit chat than that. But Pablo wasn't listening. He was too busy attentively squeezing my chest into makeshift breasts, while plaintively drawling 'Pleeeease, take me to your women,' into my shoulder.

La Paz

Andean lady in La Paz

Cerro Rico, Potosi

Miner with dynamite, Cerro Rico

Fiesta in Sucre

Aymara dancing ladies in Sucre

Religious imagery for sale in Sucre

Cactus Island, Salar de Uyuni

Southern Altiplano

Llama farmer in Picoya

Boy in Picoya

Llama herd, Picoya

Laguna Verde, Southern Altiplano

Butch Cassidy (bottom right) and the Hole in the Wall Gang

Top: Mururata in
the Cordillera Real

Right: Yungas
Cruz Trail

Top: Lake Titicaca

Middle: On
expedition,
Lake Titicaca

Bottom: Day of the
Dead, La Paz

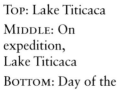

SALAR DE UYUNI

At four in the morning the town's darkness was only broken by the headlights of the occasional truck making an early start to the frontier with Chile. I waited for my lift, bundled up like an Inuit and stamping my feet to shake off the cold. After only 24 hours in the town of Uyuni I was already grateful to be leaving.

Arriving from Sucre the previous morning felt like rolling into a remote trading post on the fringes of the known universe. Bordered by the vast Salar de Uyuni, there is little in the way of human habitation beyond the town's random collection of streets. A knot of tele-communication towers in the centre looked like technology's last stand against the Andes' immobile presence beyond.

The climate adds to Uyuni's other-worldly feel. As soon as I first stepped off the bus I felt exposed under the cloudless sky, stretched so thin between far horizons that the moon's faded stencil shone on throughout the day. While the sun fixed the town in its white glare, a dry and penetrating cold still inhabited the falling shadows. Night, when it came, descended in a single, decisive stroke.

I spent my first few hours in Uyuni wandering around the busy street market that sells cheap imports and contraband from Chile. Other than this welcome distraction there seems little to advance time's snail-like passage through a day of interminable sunshine in Uyuni. Even the town's yellow and white clock tower conspired, chiming four o'clock on the hour, every hour.

I whiled away the afternoon drinking undrinkable coffee at one of the small metal tables scattered around the clock tower. There were plenty of other travellers frequenting these cafés, also killing time before catching a tour to the Salar. We must have made a strange spectacle to the locals; all of us sitting stiffly buttoned up to the chin in our warm clothes with dark glasses and fixed expressions of mild shock.

I put the shock, in part, down to the extraordinary effort required to decipher the cryptic translations on the English menus at the café. The appetisers section of my menu read as follows:

Toasts of Tuna – Cookie, gherkins, mayonnaise
Toasts of Palm – Cookie and Golf Sauce
Portion of peach with fill of Tuna
Spanish Tortilla – Pope, Onion, Cheese, French Fries
Eat National – Male Itch

The Male Itch (*Pico Macho* in Spanish), turned out to be nothing more exotic than an enormous pile of hand cut chips, sausage and onion in a rich, meaty gravy. I asked the waiter if the Pope came served in, or alongside the tortilla, but he just gave me a blank look.

First impressions of Uyuni were neatly rounded off by the hostel I ended up in. After handing over my cash at reception I was led up a flight of concrete steps to a windowless landing that flickered intermittently under a single, neon strip light. Here the effusively cheerful owner showed me, without a hint of remorse, what looked like a broom cupboard with a single metal bed folded into it.

He didn't mention the course of electric-shock treatment that was thrown in for free. The ancient electric shower unit malfunctioned, delivering a 220v shock (together with a thin dribble of piss-warm water) onto my crown. After a terrific jolt I was thrown naked onto the bathroom floor, wrapped in a mouldy shower curtain and clutching a bar of soap. I spent the rest of the evening reclining on my metal cot in total darkness (the room was too depressing to be lit), enviously listening to the muffled chatter of other contented guests, the fortunate possessors of non-lethal plumbing.

Every ex-smoker who travels in Bolivia has their breaking point – this was mine. By the time the jeep finally pulled up outside the hostel just before dawn, I had smoked most of my first packet of Bolivian filter-less cigarettes. Reputed to be composed mainly of glass shavings and sawdust, they are so rough that even the miners try not to inhale.

Bundled unceremoniously into the back of the jeep I was introduced to Santos, a Bolivian agronomist in his forties, a young Italian vet called Lilia, and our driver, José. It was José's skills that we would rely on the most, guiding us across a maze of nameless tracks and unpaved roads to the tiny village of Picoya on the far side of the Salar.

Santos, Lilia and José all worked for an Italian charity carrying out an emergency programme to improve the health of the region's llama population. Domesticated in the Altiplano for thousands of years, these oddly charismatic cameloids are still an essential source of wool, protein and transport for rural villages across the high Andes. In recent years llama have been hard hit by drought, threatening a way of life that dates back for thousands of years.

I talked my way onto this trip back in La Paz, in the hope of getting a first-hand impression of life in one of the most far-flung corners of the Altiplano. There was also a very personal motivation for finding my way into the spine of mountains that make up the *Cordillera Real*. It was in this natural frontier land between Bolivia and Chile that my father carried out much of his geological fieldwork in the 1970s and 1980s.

As we drove beyond the last orange streetlight at the edge of town the jumbled shadows of abandoned trains and carriages slipped past. They are the hulking carcasses from Bolivia's age of steam. Before the 1879 to 1883 War of the Pacific between Chile and Bolivia-Peru a railway was built between Antofogasta (then part of Bolivia) and mining centres such as Uyuni and Oruro with the help of British engineers. Owned by the Antofogasta and Bolivia railway company, Uyuni was transformed from a forlorn military outpost to a train hub with lines to Potosí, Villazon, La Paz, Arica and Giaqui on Lake Titicaca.

Many of these are old steam trains from Bolivia's last mineral boom in the early 20th century, when the country produced a quarter of the world's supply of tin. They had a further lease of life during Bolivia's disastrous Chaco war with Paraguay in 1932 and 1933 when troops were transported on the train lines to battlefields on the front line. The mining industry declined in the 1940s and the trains were dumped outside of Uyuni to become 20th century archaeological relics.

These beautiful steam locomotives, built in Germany, Britain, the United States and Japan, may have been steered into the sand over half a century ago but their corroding hulks linger on in what the locals romantically call *'el cementerio de trenes.'* Their disintegration has been accelerated by the Altiplano's harsh climate. Although looters have stripped many of them to skeletons their steel footplates remain, still worn from the footfalls of a bygone era.

Beyond the trains we pulled out into a vast, glowering emptiness. Even the stars were diminished, a few pinpricks of light struggling to pierce the gloom. The rough ground of the dirt road gave way to a smooth white surface, like opaque glass or the surface of an ice rink. I had the strange feeling that we were somehow floating above the earth, unhitched from *terra firma.*

José eased the car over criss-crossed vehicle tracks, nosing his way into the heart of the salt flats without map or compass. Dawn broke at six, gradually returning the horizon, distant mountains and a sense of belonging to the planet earth. We stopped as the sun's first soft rays tentatively felt their way across the Salar de Uyuni.

There are only a few places in the world that astronauts are said to visit because they make such an impression on them from space. The Salar, with its 10,582 square kilometres of glistening salt flats, is one of them. It is part of an extensive lake system called Lake Minchin that dried up between 30,000 and 42,000 years ago, leaving a layer of salt that in places covers over briny, subterranean waters.

Every hard kilometre travelled was worth it to reach this point, standing on a dead calm sea of burnished orange. What moved me most was the infinity of regular geometric shapes, like honey-comb, that cover the salt flats. There must be a scientific rationale for why this happens, told to explain away the sheer wonder and symmetry of the natural world. But it seemed to me as though we were being shown some greater design, as though the landscape had suddenly offered up its secrets, beautiful and cruel. Breathless and somehow lightened we ran, jumped and skidded across its surface like children.

The Aymara were similarly moved by this landscape, dreaming up a powerful creation myth to explain its existence. Three great volcanoes border the Salar, in Aymara representing the gods Thunupa, Kusina and Kuska. According to legend they were caught in a love triangle when Kuska abandoned his partner Thunupa and their baby for Kusina. Grieving the loss of her husband Thunupa's salty tears mixed with her milk, unintentionally creating the 'Salar de Thunupa.'

The future of Thunupa's Salar now hangs in the balance. These salt flats contain between 35% and 65% of the world's supply of lithium, a principle ingredient in the batteries for the mobile devices and the electric car revolution. Like the silver of the Cerro Rico, mining in the Altiplano could bring untold riches to a county still locked in poverty. The question is can it be extracted sensibly, or will Bolivia succumb to the curse of the resource rich nation: A short-lived 'white gold' rush that puts a quick buck before sustainable development and the protection of such a unique landscape.

From the Salar we drove on south for several hours, passing small islands made of fossilised coral reefs that are covered with thola brush, ichu bunch grass and native Queñua trees. Giant cacti grow up to 10 metres high here, some of them living hundreds of years. In the rainy season the Salar can be covered in a shallow film of water, giving the illusion that these islands have been returned to the sea again.

And then, beyond the southern edge of the Salar, we started to snake into the remote lands that are collectively called Sud Lípez and that are fenced on to the West by the *Cordillera Real*. It felt on this long journey as though I was suspended in motion in an open plain of burning light. The Altiplano's endless expanse of yellow grass and red earth was only broken by a few, sparse distractions: a dust devil dancing across the track ahead; a wooden cross entwined with desiccated flowers; a ripped plastic bag catching the wind in a tree. I missed the condor but saw its angled shadow flit across the open land.

The clouds were hung out in the immeasurable vast sky like ragged sheets. I grouped the smaller ones into fantastic creatures, dragons and grotesque faces. The larger banks of cumulus were solid and immobile, like forbidden continents. The frontier of jagged peaks between Bolivia and Chile seemed so bright and close in the thin air that I felt I could reach out and bind them together with a single stretch.

It wasn't hard to imagine Dad in this same landscape back in 1976, scanning the ground for tell-tale patterns of weathering that could indicate minerals lying close to the surface. Or picture him wandering through the lava flows of long dormant volcanoes to see just how heat had transformed the composition of the rock. While tracking the collision point of tectonic plates he would have been distracted by the lazy trails of glacial flows. They reminded him so much of Scotland.

And then I vividly pictured him, crouched in a dry riverbed some way up a steep slope of loose rock and brush. Dressed in leather walking boots and an orange body warmer, he was intently turning a rock over in his hands. A small pick lay beside him, glinting in the sun.

I couldn't see his face under the floppy white hat and sunglasses, but knew it shone with excitement.

This was one of those moments, after hours and days of fruitless exploration, when he found a signature rock that uncovered a secret. The sort of rock that could unlock time, whispering a hidden story into his ear about tremendous geological pressure, long past raging torrents and volcanic eruptions. He would carefully wrap these special rocks into a handkerchief and stow them away in his backpack, along with his notebook, pen and water. They became his samples, to take back to the lab for analysis. He kept some of these key stones for himself. They become markers to his distant adventures over long years exploring this dusty planet.

Once Dad took me into study to show me this collection. He reverently lined up his most favourite discoveries from his travels on a table. I remember ammonites as big as my head, a purple flush of amethyst crystals peeking out of its matt black egg. There was also a chunk of fossilised bark from a tropical tree that fitted so smoothly into the curl of my eight-year old hand.

Some of these rocks had polished cross-section to bring out their patina. The most beautiful was a heavy rock the colour of graphite with contorted folds running across the surface like waves, eels or maybe even smoke. They seemed to shimmy and shape shift under the desk lamp's slippery light. I turned it over and read the note on the back that dad had written on a splodge of white Tippex, 'Mount Isa, 1970'. The year I was born.

He seemed nervous, like this was a big moment. Once he had methodically explained where each of his rocks were from and how they were formed he asked: 'well, what do you think?' But he had already lost me.

He lost me during all those years he was away gathering his stones. 'Rocks, Dad, they are just stupid old rocks,' I replied. And that was it. A few words of finely calculated cruelty and my father's hopes for me as a prodigy geologist were crushed to powder. Dad's stones remained completely inanimate to me until he died. Now they are one of the few things I have left to remember him by.

Picoya is one of the most remote villages in the Southern Altiplano. Perched on the edge of the Salar, it is made up of a loose network of adobe houses clustered around a church with its small plaza and a football pitch. More animals than humans frequent its streets. A few scrappy dogs lay on the doorsteps, watching a couple of pigs copulate in a dusty yard. The dirt road into the village was brightened by a parade of llamas, leisurely wandering through with their awkward, upright gait, and a vague look of astonishment.

What marks Picoya out as different is the view. At over 4,300 metres above sea level the village is perched in the final range of mountains that run on their far western side down into the Atacama desert in Chile. It must be one of the most spectacular panoramas in the Altiplano, high above the Salar's gleaming salt flats and surrounding foothills. Looking out across the Salar it struck me that I was standing in one of the most remote communities on the planet.

It is hard to imagine just how the villagers of Picoya can survive at all in this environment. The only crop that is hardy enough to grow on these parched slopes is the Andes' native grain, quinoa. Llamas are the only domesticated animals that can survive the harsh conditions without intensive husbandry. If it wasn't for work in the nearby silver mine of San Cristobal there wouldn't be enough income to bring in essential provisions, such as drinking water, in the dry season.

As Santos and Lilia started carrying materials for their presentation on llama health to the schoolhouse, the villagers emerged from their fields and houses. I was immediately struck by their age. Most seemed old and infirm, their bodies bent double by decades of labour. There were a few children, energetically playing a cross between football and basketball in the school yard. But the oldest of them couldn't have been any more than twelve. The village seemed to be missing an entire generation.

The schoolhouse was no more than a long room with a few rows of benches and desks facing a large blackboard. At the opposite end there was a short wave radio and a single computer hooked up to a solar panel on the roof. The village elders perched awkwardly at the children's desks while the children themselves peered curiously through the windows. The women sat together at the back wearing the distinctive wide brimmed hats of the Quechua. Obviously unaccustomed to receiving visitors, they all maintained a hushed silence.

Santos kicked off proceedings with a lengthy introduction to their project to help improve the health of the community's llamas. Met with a wall of seemingly impenetrable reserve, he prompted the villagers to list some of their llama's most common ailments. Gradually they start calling out symptoms and the blackboard soon filled up with childlike drawings of horrific looking intestinal worms, ticks the size of thumb nails, a llama with the runs and physical deformities caused by in-breeding.

Once the group began speaking freely it quickly become evident that the villagers' concerns actually ran far deeper than just for the welfare of their animals. One farmer, named Francisco, stood up to eloquently explain how they were struggling to cope with changes in the weather. 'The rains don't fall like they used to' he said. 'Only a small amount of snow settles on the mountain of Chiwana behind the village and it melts too quickly.'

Francisco explained that the villagers were pushing further and further up the slopes to seek out enough moisture in the soil to germinate their quinoa. In doing so they are taking over the native mountain pasture that their llama depend on for food. This then weakens the llamas, making them more prone to disease and putting the community under yet more economic pressure.

Much of the southern Altiplano has been suffering from drought in recent years, with this already arid region at risk of becoming an uninhabitable desert. It seemed a cruel twist of fate that the people of this region could end up being casualties of climate change when their own contribution to the build up of greenhouse gasses is so minimal. Villagers like Francisco don't have a car, computer, iPad or heating, other than a single fire to cook on. The solar panels outside each house, installed by the municipal government, provided enough energy to run the equivalent of three light bulbs. It seems that the poorest people on the farthest corners of the planet are the first to pay for the richest's excesses.

By the time we stopped for lunch I had heard far more about the health and reproductive system of the llama than I will hopefully ever have need to make use of. Alfonso, the schoolteacher, invited us into his house, made from mud, straw and a local cactus. Here two women served up noodle soup, followed by a gargantuan dish of llama and *chuño,* the black freeze-dried potato that has been a staple in the high Andes since before the Inca.

It may have helped provide sustenance to the people of the Altiplano for centuries but *chuño* has always tasted to me like a cross between sweaty mushrooms and wet coal. I normally pride myself in being happy to eat anything, including once the boiled eyeball from a sheep's head in El Alto. But I couldn't help surveying the conical mound of glistening black lumps on my plate with similar trepidation of a mountaineer sizing up the north face of the Eiger. Santos had already warned me that it would be considered rude not to eat everything offered by our hosts.

As I tackled lunch, Alfonso cleared up the mystery of Picoya's missing generation. 'Most of the young people leave, they just don't want this life anymore, it is too hard,' he told me. 'There is plenty of quick money to be made in tourism and contraband in towns like Uyuni and Potosí with half the effort.' I nodded in sympathy, making a discreet collection point for the *chuño* beneath my upturned spoon.

Alfonso was worried that many of the community's traditions were also being lost. 'Until a few years ago many in our village went on an annual expedition with their llamas to the lower valleys to exchange salt for maize,' he told me. 'There is very little community spirit left.'

The afternoon was dedicated to a hands on demonstration. 'A good pair of balls have to be evenly coated with hair, be of equal weight and size and should hang down to the same level,' Lilia informs us as we stood in a stone paddock outside the village, intently peering at the business end of a male llama. The poor llama, pinned down by two farmers, was baying furiously at the indignity of such a public inspection. Lilia moved onto the penis: 'it has to be long, straight and free of any unnatural swellings.' We all solemnly agreed that this one was well hung and therefore good for breeding, before returning it to the rest of the cowering herd at the far end of the paddock.

Lilia, the girl from Milan who was running the afternoon's practical session, definitely added a touch of glamour to proceedings in her tight black jacket and oversized sunglasses. And yet she was in her element, wrestling llamas down to the ground to demonstrate how to safely inoculate the beasts from parasites and other common diseases.

Before long she had us all doing it and as the afternoon wore on I felt the high walls between the community and its visitors started to melt away. I had a long chat with the older men about the price of quinoa in British markets (100 times what they are paid in Uyuni) and tried to explain that there is a fair trade movement somewhere out there, set up to help farmers like them.

At the end of the day Santos and Lilia packed up, leaving the community with food supplements and treatments for their llamas. The villagers seemed to have enjoyed this distraction from the monotony of their daily lives and kept asking the same question: when are you coming back? Again and again Santos and Lilia explained that this is the end of a nine-month emergency aid programme.

Lilia shared the villagers' sense of frustration at the project's brief tenure. 'In nine months we are supposed to improve the health of 131,000 llamas, owned by 18,400 families in over a hundred communities scattered across the southern Altiplano,' she told me in the jeep back to Uyuni. 'The project was invented by a bunch of pen-pushers in Brussels, with no understanding of what the reality is on the ground. We would need twenty years working with one community like this to start making a real difference.'

I wondered if Picoya has the luxury of twenty years as we said our goodbyes and drove off in a cloud of dust. The only thing that seemed to be growing in the drought stricken land outside of the village were the crosses in the cemetery. A few miles on we passed another settlement, abandoned since the last inhabitant died there only a few years earlier. The houses were still well preserved in the drying wind and sun, but the people and their llamas had vanished.

TUPIZA

Apart from the mechanised transport it seemed little has changed in the small mining town of Tupiza on the southern edge of the Altiplano in over 100 years. The only traffic around the square was a single bus on a perpetual loop and two teenage boys doing laps on motorbikes. Maybe they had been hired by the town's mayor to give an impression of haste. I bought a cold beer and settled on a park bench amongst the central plaza's palm trees to watch young and old gossip, flirt and eavesdrop.

From here it was easy to picture the two North American *gringos* riding in off the dusty plains into town in the spring of 1908. Described as 'tall, slender, laconic and nervous, with intense gazes,' they were nattily dressed in corduroy suits, soft brimmed hats and silk handkerchiefs. In my mind's eye they tended to their horses before buying a couple of beers. I imagined them strolling over and sitting, legs stretched out after their long journey, on the wooden yellow bench beside me.

Although clearly a long way from home Butch Cassidy and the Sundance Kid's arrival in town would have barely raised an eyebrow. Tupiza at the beginning of the 20th century was at the leading edge of a tin mining boom that saw enormous wealth and power concentrated into the hands of a few families. Home to the Aramayo dynasty, which at its height owned around a quarter of all Bolivia's mines, the area attracted a constant flow of foreign engineers, entrepreneurs and financiers.

Only these two *gringos* weren't in town for legitimate business. Every month the Aramayo manager Carlos Peró set off from Tupiza on an arduous three-day trek by mule with his son and a servant, carrying the cash wages for miners in the hills to the north. On the 3rd of November 1908 the party followed the river out of town at first light to make this routine journey. They didn't notice the two men who were discreetly following behind.

Butch and Sundance ambushed and robbed Peró and his companions as they made their way through a remote mountain pass. It was to be their last heist. A few days later they were killed in a shoot-out in the desolate mining village of San Vicente, 100km from Tupiza.

Their fate inspired one of the most memorable scenes in cinematic history. The moment when Robert Redford and Paul Newman make their last bid for freedom in the classic western, *Butch Cassidy and the Sundance Kid*. The film ends in a single, sepia freeze frame of the two badly shot-up heroes, leaping out of their Altiplano hide-out to take on hundreds of Bolivian troops. Despite their being met by a thunderous volley of gunfire, I remember being left with a sliver of hope. Did they as many claim somehow manage to get away?

I have loved the tale of the two outlaws' long flight from justice to South America ever since I first saw the film as a boy. Dangerous, good-looking, and impossibly laid back, Redford and Newman were the guys I wanted to be like when I grew up. I had often wondered how men's real lives matched up to the film.

Had Butch and Sundance died in the United States I would probably have been treated to a western themed 'experience'. I might have eaten a 'Butch Burger' in the 'Hole in the Wall Saloon,' before watching heavily moustached actors re-enact the shoot-out to an audience of star struck tourists.

Wandering around Tupiza you would never have guessed that the area had such a bankable claim to fame. The tourist agencies all sold the same Wild West style horseback tours of the rugged countryside (with cowboy hat, bandana and chaps thrown in). But only one advertised *La Ruta de Butch y Sundance* in its window.

'There is nothing up there,' the girl in the cramped office plastered with pictures of faded sunsets warned me. She said the last tourists they had taken to the locations of the last robbery and the shoot-out in San Vicente had been so disappointed that they demanded their money back. Apparently the house where Butch and Sundance died had been rebuilt and the graveyard where they are supposedly buried was kept locked, 'to keep the Yankees' bad spirits from getting out.' It sounded more like a measure to prevent the tourists from getting in.

I was about to leave when she scribbled down a name and number on a slip of paper. 'You should talk to Don Félix instead,' she suggested. 'He's the town's expert on Butch and Sundance. He even has a museum dedicated to them in his house.'

Félix greeted me at the door to his home that same evening with a half smile and a crushing handshake. A portly man in his early sixties with a bristling salt and pepper moustache, he looked like a *latino* Karl Marx. Despite being dressed in tennis shoes and a nylon jacket he still carried a distinguished air that hinted at his day job. Don Félix was the principle administrator of justice in town.

At first the windowless hall that Félix ushered me into seemed cluttered with random household junk. It wasn't until my eyes adjusted to the gloom that I realised we were actually surrounded by antiques. A table was piled high with telegram machines, broken fob watches and a rolled-up leather bullet belt. Ancient agricultural tools were stacked up in the corners and a collection of Winchester rifles were splayed in a fan shape across one of the walls.

Félix stumbled over an ancient typewriter as he unfolded a couple of deck chairs for us to sit on. I noticed the long strip light on the ceiling and wondered why he hadn't turned it on. Only once we have comfortably reclined in the two creaky chairs did he pull a long cord, dramatically illuminating his hall in a spluttering neon glow. 'Welcome to my museum,' he said with a note of ceremony. I felt like the only guest at a private view.

'I knocked on the doors of all my neighbours and asked if they would look through their cupboards for antiques to fill a museum that I am planning to open,' Félix told me. Before long his house was inundated with everybody's long forgotten possessions. I haven't had time to make sense of it all,' he admitted, 'let alone move all of this stuff out of my front hall.'

Looking at the passed-down fragments of so many lives I wasn't surprised. My eyes jumped from old saddles and brass miners' lamps, to a faded photograph of Victorian women picnicking by the lazy bend of a river.

I wondered how Félix could even begin to order the view through this fractured prism into his town's distant past.

Félix indicated a large, framed portrait that didn't seem to fit the jigsaw. A black and white photo of five young men, immaculately dressed in three-piece suits with derby hats set at jaunty angles. Obviously from North America, they looked for all their finery like solemn, dangerous men. 'That's the Wild Bunch in 1900,' he explained, 'taken in Fort Worth, Texas at the height of their infamy.'

Flush from a recent heist, the gang were on a spending spree in the saloons, poker houses and bordellos in the notorious 'Hell's Half Acre' of Fort Worth when the photo was taken. They most likely posed as scrubbed-up bankers for a lark, mocking the professional classes that they both despised and secretly envied.

Félix pointed out Butch Cassidy, the mastermind behind the Wild Bunch's collection of bandits and murderers. By the time this photo was taken Butch had already spent two decades on the run, holding up banks and trains across the American West. Estimates of his overall haul during this crime spree runs to today's equivalent of more than two and a half million dollars.

I studied Butch's face, expecting to see the hard reflection of a vicious criminal. But the man who stared confidently out at me with his distinctive square jaw and the ghost of a smile looks far more likeable and relaxed than I had imagined. The real Butch may not have had Newman's rakish looks, but the outlaw's famed charm still shone through.

It is this enigmatic contradiction between Butch and his career that transformed him into such an enduring legend. Born Robert Le Roy Parker to Mormon parents in Southern Utah, Butch spurned his respectable upbringing for a life of crime. He gained a hard-earned reputation for thieving, gambling and whoring, but was also fondly remembered for his good manners, kindness to children and aversion to bloodshed. Often portrayed as a gentleman thief, Butch still rode with notorious killers like Kid Curry and at the very end of his life added murder to a long list of crime and misdemeanours.

The picture of 'the Fort Worth Five' may have cemented the Wild Bunch's place in the history of the Wild West, but it was a disaster for the men who posed for it. Félix explained that the Pinkerton Detective Agency used the photograph to circulate wanted posters with the outlaws' faces as far as Tahiti. The lawless days of the American West were fast coming to an end.

Ever restless, Butch wrote in a letter to a friend that he wanted to see more of the world. As vast as America was he felt that his home country had become too small for him. In truth his flight to South America in 1901, together with Sundance and his lover Etta Place, was driven by necessity rather than desire. Most of the Wild Bunch members who stayed behind were soon killed or imprisoned.

Félix stood up to fetch a glass of water, snapping me back across 100 years into the 21st century. As the ancient plumbing in a small washbasin in the corner of his hall groaned into life I asked how his fascination with Butch and Sundance started. 'I was a young student studying law in Potosí when the movie opened at the cinema in 1969,' he reminisced. 'I still remember the walk back from the cinema, so amazed that this Hollywood story from my home town had been forgotten for so long.'

It was the last chance that Félix had to see the film for a long time. He explained how a carelessly dropped comma in the Spanish subtitles left the ruling dictator Alfredo Ovando so enraged that he banned the film after the opening night. Newman rebukes Redford for asking 'what's Bolivia?' with the innocent enough comment, 'it's a country, stupid.' However in the Spanish version he ends up saying *es un pais estupido* (it's a stupid country). Woe betide any man who even unintentionally insults a South American dictator's country.

By the time Ovando's soldiers had stormed the cinemas to confiscate the movie reels, the story had already taken flight in Félix's imagination. When two American writers, Dan Buck and Anne Meadows, first came to Tupiza to find out what actually happened, he was quick to offer his local knowledge and contacts. 'I helped them with their research and we became good friends,' Félix told me proudly. 'The information was hidden here in town all along, in old newspaper cuttings and the municipal archives, just waiting to be discovered.'

Félix dug two red folders out of a cardboard box on the floor. Opening one of them, he began to leaf though a stack of photocopied documents from the early 20th century. 'Daniel and Anne left me these copies of all of the source material from their research,' he told me. Watching him pass his hands reverently over the spidery writings from over a century ago I wondered if Félix's hall had become a personal shrine to his own imagined past.

The folders gave an intimate account of Butch, Sundance and Etta's South American adventure. Instinctively drawn to Patagonia's remote isolation, the trio spent their first years in a four-bedroom log cabin in the Cholila valley over 1000 km south of Buenos Aires. Here they ranched peacefully, keeping 1,300 sheep and 500 head of cattle. They are even said to have brought a touch of class to the area, decorating their home with 'pictures with cane frames, wallpaper made of clippings of North American magazines, and many beautiful weapons and lassos braided from horsehair.'

Perhaps inevitably, their domestic interlude didn't last long. The Pinkerton detectives heard of their whereabouts and sent a man to Buenos Aires to alert the Argentinean authorities. Butch often dreamed of going straight but knew instinctively that it would never happen. He once wrote: 'There is always an informer around to bring the law on you. After you've started, you have to keep going, that's all. The safest thing is to keep moving all the time and spring a hold up in some new place.'

The next new place was in Villa Merced in northern Argentina in December 1905. They carried out a daring raid of the bank and escaped over the Chilean border with a posse hot on their tail. Afterwards the mysterious Etta Place was described in the Argentine newspaper *La Prensa* as: 'A fine rider, handles all classes of firearm and has an admirable male temperament.'

As this point Etta also rides out of recorded history, returning on her own to the United States. Butch and Sundance pushed on into Bolivia, working for a while in the Concordia tin mine south of La Paz before riding into Tupiza in November 1908.

I walked out of Tupiza at dawn the following morning towards the pass on *Huaca Huanusca* mountain where Butch and Sundance ambushed Carlos Peró. Following the river I marvelled at the crumbling ranges of fluted sandstone that tower over the valley floor, like an army of giant sentinels looming over the deep canyons of fallen shadow within.

No wonder the outlaws felt so at home in South America. Butch once wrote that the Andes were 'a treeless jungle of badlands, peaks, ridges and minor valleys that could easily be mistaken for southern Utah.'

By the time I reached the hamlet of Salo, the afternoon had turned hot and airless. The Aramayo hacienda where Peró spent the night had been long pulled down and replaced by a school. But a row of single roomed, adobe houses with tiny windows remained. Perhaps it was in one of these that Butch and Sundance spent the night, rising before sunrise to get ahead of their intended victims.

The truck driver who I had hitched a lift from dropped me at a sharp curve in the hills. At the road edge the ground fell steeply away to a narrow river snaking through a deep gorge. I could just make out the faint trace of a path threading its way through the ravine. This was the old route that Carlos Perós' party rode along by mule from Salo a century ago. I imagined Butch and Sundance lying in wait for them, watching their slow approach through binoculars.

As I scrambled nervously down the steep slope towards the trail I suddenly felt very exposed. It had obviously been a long time since anyone had walked into this mountain pass. I hadn't told anyone were I was headed so if something happened I would just simply vanish from the face of the earth. I couldn't imagine a more futile end, the coroner registering an 'accidental death whilst in hot pursuit of two ghosts from the past.'

I realised that I was being drawn onto the same obsession that had gripped Félix and his friends Dan Buck and Anne Meadows. At one point in her book *Digging up Butch and Sundance* Anne Meadows questions the single-minded fascination with outlaws that brought her to the point of financial ruin. How, she wonders, had her entire universe come to 'revolve around a time and place that no longer exists.'

The spot where Butch and Sundance ambushed Peró and his companions was unchanged; a pleasant stretch of river below a rocky bluff, dotted with cacti and a few gnarled trees. I watched a brilliant hummingbird dart with unerring precision between delicate yellow and red desert flowers. The girl in the tourist agency was right, there really was nothing to see. And yet there was something about retracing Butch and Sundance's steps that brought them back to life for me.

Standing on the exact location of the heist I could vividly picture the moment when 'two individuals with rifles, one thin and tall, the other fat' confronted Peró. Sundance stood back while Butch, acting 'in a very menacing manner,' liberated Peró of his payroll of crisp banknotes, together with his best mule. Peró and his companions were left unharmed – it wasn't long before they had raised the alarm.

From the *Huaca Huanusca* pass the two bandits fled back along the tortuous path towards Tupiza, frustrated by what turned out to be a comparatively meagre down payment on the miners' wages (they netted the equivalent of ninety thousand dollars rather than the half a million they had anticipated). They struck back north again outside of Tupiza, reaching the desolate mining village of San Vicente at sundown on the 6th of November.

The eye witness accounts of what really happened next are a far cry from the Hollywood version. Cleto Bellot, San Vicente's chief administrative officer, offered Butch and Sundance a room for the night but grew suspicious of the two edgy *gringos*. When they gave him some money and asked him to fetch beer and sardines he went for the law instead.

Earlier that day a four-man posse of soldiers and a police captain from Uyuni (hardly the swarm of Bolivian soldiers in the 1969 film) had ridden into the village on the lookout for the culprits of the Aramayo robbery. As soon as Bellot told them of the heavily armed gringos, they rushed around to the building where Butch and Sundance were resting.

Butch let off the first shot with his colt pistol from the doorway, killing the leading soldier. The other lawmen scurried for cover and returned fire on the building. Trapped in a single room with no way out the outlaws held out until around midnight, when 'three desperate screams' were heard coming from inside. The Bolivians staked out the building throughout the bitterly cold night until first light, when they gingerly entered. Inside they found two dead bodies.

Butch was stretched out on the floor and Sundance was sitting on a bench behind the door, with his arms around a large ceramic jar. Both had gunshot wounds in their arms and single rounds in their heads. From the position of the bodies the witnesses concluded that Butch had shot the badly wounded Sundance, before turning the gun on himself.

Félix gave me a copy of the detailed inventory of the two men's worldly possessions. These include the Aramayo mule carrying the miners' wages, enough arms and ammunition to start a small war, ponchos, binoculars, a notebook and the silver fob watch that Butch had bought from Tiffany's in New York, before setting sail to Argentina. In the true spirit of Bolivian officialdom the police captain promptly absconded to Uyuni with the lot. It took the Aramayo company months in court before they recovered their money, not to mention their adventure-prone mule.

As for Butch and Sundance's remains, their bodies were wrapped in blankets and hastily interred in an unmarked grave in San Vicente's cemetery. Never properly identified, the Bolivian government didn't even get around to issuing death certificates until 1910, 'for the two men whose names (were) unknown.'

But did Butch and Sundance really die in San Vicente? Lingering doubts, hinted at by the film's ambiguous ending, have added further mystique to the story. Félix showed me a record of two other heavily armed Americans, calling themselves Ray Walters and Frank Harry Murray, who were detained and released outside Tupiza around the time of the shoot-out.

Could they really have been Butch and Sundance giving authorities the slip? And what about the rumours that one of the dead robbers was actually a Chilean accomplice? Or that Butch swapped clothes with a slain soldier and crawled out of San Vicente unscathed?

In the decades after 1908 Butch was spotted all over North America, often digging up buried loot. He is reported to have become, amongst other professions, a travelling salesman, lumber dealer, banker, miner, civil engineer even a Hollywood extra. Most credible of all is the account by his own sister Lula Parker Betenson of his turning up at her house in 1925 in a shiny, black Ford for a chat and a slice of blueberry pie. She swore that he died peaceably of pneumonia in the northwest some years later.

Sundance's alleged career paths after San Vicente are even more colourful. He has been linked to numerous murders and was said to have sold mineral water, led a cult, joined the Mexican revolution with Etta and fought against the Turks in the First World War. Much like Elvis, Butch and Sundance became the legends that nobody wanted to die.

Back in Tupiza I decided to track Félix down again in the hope that he could shed some fresh light on the enduring mystery surrounding the outlaws' last days. I found him working in his office in the grandly named *'Palacio de Justicia.'* The shelves in the small room on the top floor of a dilapidated townhouse were groaning under the weight of case files. Félix spends most of his time dealing with disputes between neighbours or marital strife. 'It's a big headache,' he sighed with a careworn look.

Happy to be distracted, we took a stroll to the municipal museum in the central plaza but we made slow progress as Félix stopped to shake hands and exchanged pleasantries with practically every passer by. Even the local policeman took a break from directing traffic to inquire after the progress of his divorce through the courts. It struck me that Butch and Sundance were a welcome escape from his everyday embroilment in the mundane dealings of small town life.

Tupiza's municipal museum was in an even worse shape than Félix's front hall. Much of it was given over to a collection of strange, saucer shaped stones. The curator told me she thought that they were the remains of a meteor storm that had fallen on the desert long before she started working there. Félix gently chided her for mixing up the uniforms from the wars of the Pacific and the Chaco (conflicts more than 50 years apart).

I was ushered over to a glass cabinet in the corner housing an old colt revolver and a skull with a hole neatly punched through its forehead. 'This,' Félix told me, 'is the proof that was supposed to lay the whole matter to rest, but never did.' In 1991 Buck and Meadows led an expedition to exhume the remains of what they thought was the Sundance Kid from the cemetery at San Vicente. They thought the skull they found, damaged from what looked like a bullet hole, was a dead give away.

After extensive DNA analysis a forensic team in Germany ended up matching the remains to a German engineer called Gustav Zimmer, who had blown himself up while defrosting dynamite on his stove. Félix was contrite for his part in this bizarre case of mistaken identity: 'I feel sorry for old Zimmer,' he lamented. 'What would he have said if he knew his bones were going to be dug up, sent all the way to Germany and then returned to this glass case?'

I pointed out that without Butch and Sundance's remains, there is no actual proof that the outlaws died in Bolivia. Félix admitted that we will never know for sure what happened to them. 'The bodies were laid on top of each other at San Vicente's cemetery,' he said. 'We'll never find them.'

But Félix had an ace card up his sleeve. He pulled several neatly folded photocopied pages from an inside jacket pocket and spread them out on the glass cabinet. They were a collection of letters written by the United States' consulate, on behalf of Sundance's lover Etta Place, to the Bolivian authorities.

The letters repeatedly ask for official confirmation that it was Butch and Sundance who died in San Vicente. The last one is dated 1912, four years after they disappeared. If Butch and Sundance had made it home from Bolivia, Etta would never have pressed her consulate to send these letters,' Félix told me. 'Poor Etta,' he added, 'she must have been so desperate to find out what had happened to them but she never got a straight answer.'

Looking at Félix hunched so intently over the papers, I couldn't help but ask why a man of the law had dedicated so much of his time to a pair of thieves. 'I still can't work out if they are bandits or heroes,' he answered, without looking up. Then he turned, stared me hard in the eyes and said: 'I have never hurt or killed a man, except in self-defence and have never stolen from the poor but only from rich corporations well able to support my requisitions.' This, he explained, was Sundance's defence to an English friend after admitting to his true identity.

I left Félix on the steps of the town hall with a very different image of what, in truth, was an inglorious end to the colourful careers of Butch and Sundance. I felt confident that, despite all the rumours, Butch and Sundance never escaped from Bolivia. There wasn't even a Hollywood ending for the *'bandidos yanquis.'* After years of evading capture they ended up being cornered by a few soldiers, choosing to perish by their own hands rather than face Bolivian justice. They died exhausted and desperate men, buried in a shallow grave in the Altiplano's shivering heights.

Perhaps the real Butch and Sundance could never have lived up to their big screen personas. And yet they remain my fallen heroes all the same. Their story is just sharper edged now. Their lives so much more human, and finite, than the tale that I had grown up with.

Fallen heroes. Dad's career in geology began with exploring the burns and craggy bens around Knockie in Inverness-shire as a child. By his late teens he had graduated to full on mountain climbing, tackling many craggy peaks in the Scottish Highlands and the Alps. I still marvel at the old black and white photos I have of my father with his young friends, perched on razor edged peaks with looped coils of thick hessian rope across their shoulders. Dad's wooden handled axe from these days is in the attic, as long as my arm and twice as heavy.

His passion for rocks grew out of scrambling over Scotland's fractured geological past. He had a feel for the properties of rocks such as basalt, sandstone and granite long before he went on to study them. How some rock like the gabbro of the Black Cullin is tactile and easy to climb, while basalt is murderously slippery when wet. Knowing rocks so intimately and wanting to understand how they are formed was a natural leap for Dad. The course of his life was set by the time he left Gordonstoun and set his sights on studying Geology at McGill University in Montreal.

He met my American mother Lucy at a Geography class at McGill, thanks to them both being left handed. The desks were so cramped that they were forced to sit next to each other so they could write without knocking elbows. They were both running away from a conventional life and after university eloped to Australia to start a new life together. They travelled by assisted passage as Dad had been offered work in Mount Isa Mines. Married in a registry office in Sydney, much to chagrin of both their families, they started married life in a prefab with a tin roof in the Outback, some five hundred miles from the coast.

Dad once showed me a couple of photos of the shoe-box white house with a tiny garden and picket fence holding out the faded desert behind. It must have been such a shock for both of them, especially my mother who had grown up in cool, wooded seclusion in New

England. She remembers their windows being sealed shut and said the house was turned into a pressure cooker every afternoon by the heat. Keeping busy was the only distraction – she would pass the time making oddly fitting clothes with a hand crank sewing machine and baking endless loaves of fresh bread.

Meanwhile Dad threw himself into his first proper job as a geologist writing back to his parents a detailed, and admittedly at times rather dry, account of his work, care of the Staff Mess:

"I am working in the mine surface geology department which is responsible for working out the geological structure of the mine and the area running about 20 miles north and south of the mine where we hope there are workable deposits. I am responsible for observations and drill holes from surface. There is another branch who do all the underground geology work. Most of the mine workings are underground – down to 3000 feet below the surface.

The geology is exceedingly complex and there is a lot that is not understood. There is one open pit that is finished and being filled in (500 feet deep) and they are just opening another. They mine two distinct ores. Copper ore and silver-lead-zinc ore. The copper ore is concentrated and smelted here. The lead –silver ore is separated from the zinc which is also smelted here, while the lead-silver is concentrated here and sent to Townsville for further concentration and then sent to England for separation and refining. The by-product of the Townsville concentration goes to the U.S.A where cobalt is extracted.

Much of NW Queensland is suffering from serious drought and the countryside is desperately barren. All red rock boulders and gravel. The countryside is very broken in small steep isolated hills and land sharp ridges of almost bare rock. Further east the hills die out and the land is flat and bare. It is virtually desert, although a few cattle manage to survive somehow. The heat is appalling in the early afternoon. There is no shade, the sun beats down from directly above and the rocks are almost too hot to touch. I spent my first day out in the field yesterday and wished I was working in the underground sector!"

After quickly proving himself at Mount Isa Dad was promoted into the exploration group of Kennecott Mines and posted with my mother to New Guinea. It was here in the late 60s and early 70s that he cut his teeth as an exploration geologist. He went on long expeditions into the jungles of the Star Mountains, tracing mineral trails in river sediments in the Sepic and Maprik areas. He was so hardy on these trips that his colleagues used to joke that all he needed to survive was a case of dog food and a pouch of pipe tobacco.

Once he decided the best way to give up smoking was to be dropped off by helicopter without any tobacco, for six weeks of self-imposed cold turkey. Three days later there was an emergency call to base from his field radio. The helicopter had to be scrambled and sent looking for a thin plume of smoke rising from the jungle. It marked the spot were dad was waiting for a package of tobacco to be dropped into his camp. He told me that the American pilots had come straight from Vietnam and would go anywhere they were asked to because they were so happy not to be shot at any more. He described being dropped by helicopter onto a river bed through a narrow break in the rainforest, the ends of the rotors literally skimming the tree branches as they descended.

His team had to take an armed government patrol guard or *kiap* with them when they went to the more remote areas on the Indonesian border, as many of the local tribes had never seen white men before. Dad would trade machetes and salt for bows and arrows, statues and beautifully carved ceremonial shields. The sawn-off crocodile prow of a dug-out canoe is propped up in the corner of my sitting room.

One of Dad's letters to his parents, dated April 29th 1969, gives an idea of how pioneering these exploratory trips were, even if he was a foot soldier for that age old colonial project to exploit minerals regardless of the human cost. As one of the first white people to travel into some of the more remote areas I can't help but wonder what responsibility Dad inadvertently carries for the assimilation and destruction of such incredible diverse peoples.

"One of the remarkable things about New Guinea is the number of completely different tribes with completely different mentality and even appearance within a fairly small area. There are something like 75 distinct languages and most people are or were traditionally enemies with their neighbours in the next valley, even through sometimes they are the same tribe and speak the same language. Only ten miles from my last camp is an area where the people are still cannibals and still raid into neighbouring

valleys for meat (human). I shall possibly be going there later – with police and not walking far from the helicopter. But actually once you can make contact with people like that they are usually quite friendly towards a white man because of his obvious tremendous power (evidence – the helicopter). They tend to regard him as an extra–terrestial anyway, provided he doesn't have an axe to grind and try and turn them from their traditional ways and beliefs. We can travel safely where the administration officers would get shot at because they know that the government wants to change their way of life"

Meanwhile my mother Lucy braved poisonous spiders and overly inquisitive natives in a small wooden house on stilts in Goroka. Escaping from her privileged upbringing, she took to her radically new environment with characteristic energy and good humour. An ardent liberal and feminist she took exception to the division of labour amongst locals. On one occasion she was driving into the local village when she spotted a proud tribesman walking to the market with his wife trailing behind carrying all the fruit they were going to sell on her back. Deciding to give her a lift mum screeched to a halt, piled the lady and all her clobber into the back of the car and tore past her astonished husband in a cloud of dust.

I have a photo of Mum looking impossibly young, barefoot wearing a white shirt and rolled up trousers. She never did cope very well in the heat. She is sitting on a bench in front of a bamboo house, surrounded by scantily clad highland women, girls and boys. She looks relaxed, although I know from her strained smile that she is very aware she is sticking out like a sore thumb. A long-haired pig lies asleep at her feet. I think she must be pregnant with me in this image and she told me that I was the first 'white bump' that the locals had ever seen.

She gave birth to me in a tiny field hospital in Papua New Guinea's Eastern Highlands in 1970. I was a breach baby with the umbilical cord wrapped around my neck and so Mum had to have an emergency Caesarean a month early. She remembered my father sitting for a long time in silence at the bottom of my crib with an unlit pipe in his mouth, grinning from ear to ear. Dad dashed out to buy cigars for all his colleagues and then headed back into the jungle within a few days for another six-week field trip.

It was this brutal work schedule of six weeks away in the jungle, followed by two weeks back home, that set the pattern for family life. As a baby I freaked out every time this strange man walked back into our house. My mother confided in a letter to a friend that; 'Jamie is a great comfort to me when Nigel is gone, the house doesn't feel so lonely: though Nigel and I both feel that he is missing so much by being away.'

Dad also found it hard to adjust to the new reality. He would still try to listen to his beloved classical music on a turntable with a stylus that jumped if anyone walked across the wooden floor. Once he fell asleep on the floor with a set of headphones, playing his favourite composer Bach's piano Preludes and Fugues. Mum crept up and silently swapped it for Nellie the Elephant. Year's later she still giggled at the mix of shock and horror on dad's face when she maxed out the volume.

From PNG we barely kept pace with my father's work placements in obscure corners of the world. While my mother got on with the daily grind of bringing up a young family, Dad was exploring uncharted areas of the Amazon rainforest, or tapping rocks 5,000 metres up in the Andes.

There came a point in Dad's life when no amount of exotic travel and high-altitude adventure could make up for what he was missing out on at home. His long absences eventually eroded their marriage to the point at which my parents divorced when I was nine years old. Dad was posted to Rio de Janeiro where he met and married his second wife Rosanna. They had a daughter, Claudia and lived in Holland and Denver in the States before settling in South America. Dad lived the rest of his life with his family in Chile and Brazil.

Somehow during this long unravelling I lost my thread. The boyhood narrative that my dad would one day stop adventuring and finally come home never came to pass. For a long, long time I trusted he would breeze back into our lives for good. I imagined him arriving late one night to gather me and my brother in his arms, kiss my mum and tell us he was back to stay. In a way I am still waiting, like Etta, for a shadow to flit past the window, or the scrape of a boot on the front step.

I often dream up the questions I would ask on his return. What did you really find on your travels? Did you miss us? Were you happy? How did you lose your way back to us on those long journeys away?

TIWANAKU

The dingy office where I had arranged to meet Lindsay, above Plaza San Francisco back in La Paz, had seen better days. An old sofa pushed against the wall under the window was covered in sleeping bags, car parts and a stuffed caiman with a broken tail. The spare tyre for a Toyota jeep lay on the floor. Next to it stood a surveying theodolite on tall, metal legs. You could guess from the floral blooms of mould in the coffee cups that Lindsay's work kept him away from his desk for most of the time.

I had met first met Lindsay propping up a bar in one of La Paz's many late night drinking dens the night before. I was looking for an archaeologist to show me around the ancient city of Tiwanaku and he certainly looked the part. Unshaven with long dark hair swept back beneath a broad-rimmed felt hat he was dressed in a loose shirt, beaten up leather jacket, jeans and a surprisingly shiny pair of cowboy boots. All that was missing was the bull-whip and a busty assistant in permanent need of rescue.

Lindsay was lured to La Paz and away from a comfortable life teaching archaeology in Australia a decade ago. When I asked him why, he explained, rather grandly, that he had turned his back on the Old World.

'Everyone back home is governed by endless rules and a culture of fear to keep them plugged into their entertainment systems.' he told me. There was also a professional incentive for re-locating. Starved of funding to excavate its countless ruins, Bolivia remains one of the last frontiers for archaeological exploration in South America. By the end of the night he had promised to take me the very next day to one of 'several lost cities' that he knew of in the Altiplano.

After finding and lighting up a loose cigarette Lindsay continued to rifle through his desk, running through a mental checklist of things to take on our trip to Lake Titicaca. 'Car keys, driver's license, jerry can, military maps, GPS,' he mumbled to himself, 'Ah yes, mustn't forget Jesus.' Pushing a stack of papers off his desk he revealed a long machete in a stitched leather sheath. He picked it up nonchalantly and waved it at me as though it were a letter opener. 'If anyone gives us any trouble on the road I'll just introduce them to my old friend here,' he said.

The image of this hardy adventurer was softened by one incongruous detail: a small straw picnic hamper perched on the edge of the desk. As we left he scooped it up under his arm, a food parcel made up by his loving Bolivian wife. Under the corn beef and crackers she had tucked away napkins and Swiss chocolate, to ease the hardships of our excursion into the wild.

'La Paz is a town of grave robbers and treasure hunters,' he warned me as we loaded up a battered jeep with provisions on the busy street outside of his office. Every new archeological discovery in his patch of the Andes was followed by an ungodly rush to get hold of the loot by treasure hunters and academic institutions. Most of it ended up abroad, in the hands of private collectors or museums. As a result, Lindsay has had to keep the locations of his finds very close to his chest. Much of his work was dedicated to trying to keep Bolivia's archaeology within Bolivia.

We had to pick up Lindsay's dog before we left town. When I asked what breed it was I was soon corrected: 'Actually Merlin is a wolf.' Sure enough he emerged from his flat with a large rangy creature with gleaming eyes and shaggy brown hair that fell off in clumps every time I dared to stroke him. A wild mountain dog from the high Andes, Merlin was rescued from hunters when he was a puppy.

Merlin filled the entire back of the jeep, whining and dribbling with excitement down the back of my neck. I felt like resigning myself to the moment by winding down the window and yelling 'scoobidoobiedoo' as we drove out of the city and onto the vanishing ribbon of road that sliced the open plain in two.

When the Spanish conquistadors stumbled across the remains of the pre-Incan civilization of Tiwanaku in Bolivia's northern Altiplano all memory of its inhabitants had long since faded. The locals at Tiwanaku said the enormous stone temples, pyramids, portals and 30ft megaliths covered in anthropomorphic gods outside of their village had been built in a single day. With anything of value already long since looted (the pyramids were apparently once coated in gold plate) the Spanish destroyed what they could and moved on.

The extraordinary sophistication of this ancient civilisation has continued to baffle all who visit. The famous *Puerta del Sol* in the temple of *Kalasasaya* at the western end of Tiwanaku is thought to map out the same Roman calendar that we use today. Mummies have been discovered which show that complex surgical procedures were practised, such as 'trephination' to relieve swelling on the brain. No one knows how 132 ton andesite blocks were transported from over 60 kilometres away to build the temple of Pumapunka.

Lindsay warned me as we drove through the limitless horizon of the Altiplano that I would need an open mind to understand Tiwanaku. 'Out here,' he said between grinding gear changes and bouts of hysterical whining from Merlin, 'you can push almost any idea and watch the ripples get wider and wider.'

With no written record and less than 5% of the site actually excavated, Tiwanaku has inspired all number of outlandish theories. Some say that it was actually a pre-historic port city on the vanished continent of Lemuria in the South Pacific. The author Erich von Daniken has taken a further leap of imagination, claiming that Tiwanaku was once the earthly spaceport for alien visitors.

The truth may still be out there, but the real history of Tiwanaku is probably a lot more mundane. Archaeological evidence points to a culture that developed gradually from some two thousand years BC on the shores of Lake Titicaca. It grew into a sophisticated state that at its height stretched into modern day Chile, Argentina and Peru. For all its longevity the Tiwanaku culture collapsed suddenly in the 12th and 13th centuries, a victim of drought and political unrest.

We pulled into a car park lined with kiosks selling bottles of Fanta, Coca Cola and assorted cigarette cartons dangling from looped string. From outside the chain-linked fence, there to keep out the un-ticketed masses, the site looked like a large enclosure of derelict ground with a low hill covered in pale, yellowing grass.

I had seen this place, under the cover of darkness, once long before. When I was last in Bolivia I joined thousands of revellers at the Aymara New Year celebrations in Tiwanaku, held every year on the Southern Hemisphere's winter solstice, the 21st of June. We survived the freezing winter temperatures huddled around makeshift fires, dancing and playing music. I remember the first rays of sunlight stroking our upheld fingers at dawn in a moment of sublime, collective relief.

The main museum was closed for repairs, having suffered structural problems within a few years of opening (so much for progress). So we wandered through the visitor centre's endless collection of ceramics. I feigned interest for Lindsay's sake, being strictly of the 'when you've seen one earthenware pot you've seen them all' school of archaeology.

The low hill that I had seen from the car park turned out to be the remains of Akapana, a seven stepped stone pyramid that is being partially reconstructed on one side. We walked to the top and gazed into a sunken depression scattered with stone blocks in the centre. This was once an enormous stone platform, inlaid with the ancient symbol of the Andean cross and filled with water. Astronomers would peer into the cross's dark reflection to track the constellations across the night sky.

The poetry of this image alone was enough to bridge millennia and stir Tiwanaku back to life for me. Scanning the broad plain of nondescript land that surrounded us I tried to picture how Tiwanaku might have once looked. Outside of the religious centre, hundreds of families of artisans and farmers would have lived in circular adobe huts. It is thought that Lake Titicaca's shimmering waters, a distant mirage away from the ruins now, reached the city's limits in ancient times. Totora reed boats must have constantly plied these waters as the Tiwanaku State used the lake to extend its influence across the northern Altiplano.

An intense debate rages around whether Tiwanaku was a religious and administrative centre or a large urban settlement in its own right. Lindsay is firmly of the view that Tiwanaku was once a city, supporting anywhere between 30,000 and 300,000 people. He explains that the elite priests and nobles lived in the stone temples and palaces and were separated from the rest of the city's residents by a deep moat of running water.

Tiwanaku's leaders are thought to have used religion, rather than military might, to rule their lands. Wandering around the temple remains I was struck by how exclusive they would have been with their high walls and closed inner sanctums. What better way for the powerful few, with their privileged access to the Gods, to ensure the devotion of the masses.

So just who were these powerful few who so creatively sought to dominate Tiwanaku society? The large sandstone megaliths depicting Viracocha, the pan-Andean God of creation, offer up one intriguing possibility. All of the figures of Viracocha share one striking similarity: facial hair. What makes their already impressive moustaches and goatees totally extraordinary is the fact that to this day Andean men are unable to grow beards.

Could these deities have been inspired by visitors from across the seas? Some say the faces on these Tiwanaku statutes look like Viking warriors. Lindsay thinks their dress and stance is more similar to Phoenician traders of the time. It is very possible that long before the arrival of the Spanish, trading links were established between the Americas and the peoples of distant continents. Far from 'discovering' the New World in 1492, the conquistadors were possibly just the first to claim possession of everything that lay in their path.

From Tiwanaku we turned onto a back road that wound past a string of farming communities towards Lake Titicaca. We were trying to reach a remote peninsula where Lindsay had found countless ruins, including the footprint of a sunken temple. Only first we had to find our way across a deep river that ran between us and the stretch of land with the remains.

We spotted what looked like a small bridge on the satellite map on the laptop, but nothing seemed to match up with the country that we were driving through. The coordinates that I had punched into my GPS handset indicated that we still had to cover several hundred miles of Tajikistan. Modern navigation systems aren't designed for dyslexics.

We stopped in a village to ask directions but the drab houses surrounding a crumbling concrete and steel playground seemed deserted. A door creaked open and an old man emerged onto his front step, his face still in deep shadow. When I asked him where we were he said 'Asunta' going on to clarify that this was one of three Asuntas, pointing in opposite directions to indicate where the other two lay.

Just as we were working up something of a rapport Merlin jumped out of the back of the jeep to deposit a large turd in the centre of the plaza, before tearing chunks out of the village's resident dog. By the time we managed to get our hound under some semblance of control community relations had taken a considerable dent.

The old man retreated back into his house and a crowd of four angry looking villagers gathered on the plaza corner. Fearing that this could get ugly we quickly retreated to the relative security of the jeep. We must have looked fairly pathetic, sitting in the front of a stationary vehicle in the middle of their village, clutching our lap-tops and GPS systems.

The youngest of the group, a teenager in a shell suit approached us holding a lit cigarette in his hand. He wanted to know why we had come to steal their cattle and sheep. I tried to explain that we were just lost tourists but he looked at me vacantly. Tourism was obviously a novel concept in these parts.

Lindsay managed to defuse the situation by explaining that he was an archaeologist and that we are merely trying to get to the village of Belenyaye to inspect a sunken temple. He asked if anyone could direct us to the bridge across the river to the peninsula. The boy told us that there was a turn off to our elusive bridge, back the way we had already come.

As we hammered back down the dirt road my companion took to swearing profusely in a rapid-fire mix of Spanish and English in-between swigs from his hip flask; 'I know the f****** turn off is on *este camino*, I just don't know where in *el nombre del dios* the f*** it is.' I tried to focus on the green (all I could make out was green) satellite photo on the laptop while Merlin, for once, sat silent in the back. I couldn't tell if this is because he was feeling contrite, or just supremely content. All he was missing was a good shag to round off the perfect day.

For all of our technology it took a bicycle with a punctured tyre to get us over the bridge. We stopped to ask a man by the side of the road pushing his bike for directions to Belenyaye. It turned out that he lived exactly where we were headed and wouldn't have been able to make it home before nightfall on foot without a lift.

I hauled his bicycle onto the roof and he sat up front, directing us down a series of tracks between fields of quinoa and potatoes. At one point the ground was so rough that a couple leading a donkey laden with firewood overtook us. 'Follow us,' the woman called cheerfully as they passed us.

By the time Lindsay had found a familiar road we were both ready for a break. He pulled over in a remote valley with a spectacular view over Lake Titicaca and switched off the engine. A single fishing boat flicked a triangle of brilliant red sail onto the lake's blue waters. I watched it catch the breeze for a few moments, its progress slowed by the crushing scale of the Andes beyond.

The valley that we stood in was just as beguiling. A wide arc of hills ran down to a small bay that looked straight out past the tall, circular reed banks to the island of Pariti. Virtually every inch of the valley's slopes were covered in stone buildings and crumbling terraces from the Tiwanaku period. But these buildings, complete with streets and steps, weren't for the living.

'Welcome to the valley of the dead,' Lindsay said with an expansive sweep of his arm and a mawkish grin. 'It was here that they brought the mummified bodies along the old road that runs through the hill behind us.' We took a stroll through this silent city. The tombs may have long since been robbed of their contents but the place still felt occupied. It was as though the stones were watching.

'No wonder the locals won't live here,' I thought to myself with an involuntary shiver as we walked back to the jeep. The ground was covered in charred stumps of burnt grass from a recent electrical storm. A flicker of dry lightning licked the horizon and a gust of wind whipped up a sudden flurry of whitecaps on the lake. The whole landscape seemed to be leaning in, pressing us on before nightfall.

By the time we finally reached the village of Belenyaye it was pitch dark. We had to shine the jeep's headlights onto a raised area of ground where the sunken temple was supposedly buried. It was so cold outside that Merlin, the incredibly hardy Andean wolf-dog, preferred to stay in the back of the jeep.

I followed Lindsay into the biting wind, the red burn of his cigarette trailing on ahead of me. He pointed out the grassed-over tops of the temple walls. All around us there were charred remains of small fires with burnt gifts for the Earth Goddess the Pachamama. This temple may have fallen into disuse thousands of years ago but it was still a place of worship.

My guide knelt down to inspect a few bleached bones, together with some old broken glass bottles sticking out of the ground. 'Definitely human remains,' he said with the indifferent tone of someone used to handling the earth's macabre offerings. 'Judging from the age of the bottles I would say that this dates back to around the 1920s.'

Human sacrifice has been used in the Andes for centuries, mainly to bring rain in times of drought. I'd even heard rumours of it still being relatively common-place today. One of La Paz's most popular urban myths is that every major road or apartment block has a body set in concrete beneath it to placate the spirits.

Lindsay stood up and, scraping his heel across the unyielding soil, told me that he hoped to find ancient statues below our feet. Even in the darkness the headlights caught a glint in his eyes. 'This is a once in a lifetime opportunity,' he said. 'If you don't make a big find as an archaeologist, you don't make a name for yourself,'

Like Tiwanaku could this temple have been at the heart of a large, urban centre with a highly organized system of labour? Certainly every inch of available land on the peninsula we had driven through was covered with crumbling terraces, drainage canals and ruined houses.

It was a surreal moment: standing on a scrappy bit of ground at nightfall with the remains of what might be a lost city beneath our feet. I felt like we should be in pith helmets and white breeches. The only difference from those 19th century explorers is that having found El Dorado we got to jump back into a warm jeep and nibble on home baking and Swiss chocolate.

Lindsay's ultimate ambition was to see the entire peninsula named an archaeological park, in recognition of its remarkable human heritage. 'This is all about pride,' he said, his voice straining in the wind. 'For too long the people of the Altiplano have been seen as a bunch of poor Indians in need of Prospero's art of European improvement. Few realize that they are actually the direct descendants of one of the greatest civilisations of the ancient world.'

ISLA DEL SOL

The jetty thronged with fellow pilgrims on the 8:30am boat trip from Copocabana to *Suriqui*, Lake Titicaca's Island of the Sun. I joined the crowd as we were herded, like sleepy cattle, into three wooden launches. Easing out across the lake in matching orange life vests, it felt like we were surreal commuters, off to work on ourselves on this island of spiritual illumination.

The *Isla del Sol* or Island of the Sun has long been a powerful draw for pilgrims to worship. In pre-Columbian times visitors flocked from across the Andes to walk the island's rocky spine to the spot where the Sun and the Moon were believed to have first emerged after a time of darkness and flood. The island's fame peaked in the Incan era, when it was also credited for being the birthplace of the empire's dynasty of 'divine' rulers, Manco Capac and his sister Mama Occlo.

The idea of following this 'sacred route of the Incas,' had long caught my imagination. Like so many before me I was drawn by the idea of following such a well-trodden path, a journey with a fixed horizon and clear purpose. But most of all I wanted to walk my own homage to my father through the high Andes alone.

The first sight of the *Isla del Sol* heightened our collective sense of anticipation. The island's gentle sweep of rolling hills seemed the only anchor point of firm land on the lake's shimmering expanse of brilliant blue. From a distance I could just about make out the spindly lines of crumbling stone terraces that scored the island's slopes.

Before long we were pulling into a small harbour with a staircase of Incan stone steps climbing steeply from the tiny beach to a high ridgeline above. Weighed down with excessive camping gear, I embarked on the long, breathless trudge up this stairway to the heavens. Only a farmer flailing a reluctant donkey with a wiry stick and two dangerously unstable *latina* girls pulling a pink dolly-trolley in high heels, matched my pace.

Stumbling badly at the top I almost tripped headlong into a deep well, lined with smooth, regular stone. It would have made for an ungainly end to this journey: man and backpack wedged into the bottom of the sacred well where Incan pilgrims once cleansed themselves before their trek across the island.

Many of today's visitors to the island were seeking out a different kind of watering hole. Signs throughout the village of Yamani advertised cold beer, organic coffee, vegetarian cuisine and 'exclusive terrace views' of the lake. The locals were obviously long accustomed to tending thirsty tourists, together with their animals and crops, with even-handed patience.

On the outskirts of the village I caught sight of the dark outline of another nearby island. This is the Island of the Sun's smaller sister, the *Isla de la Luna* or Island of the Moon. Long revered as the spot where Viracocha called the moon into being the Tiwanaku people constructed a major temple on the island. The Inca followed on with their own temple, together with the nunnery of Mamakuna, built between 1450 and 1532.

Much less popular with travellers, I visited La Isla de la Luna with my friend James when I was living in Bolivia. There was no public transport onto it back then and we had to hire a private launch to take us there. We landed fully equipped with a flimsy tent, biscuits and a bottle of wine. It only crossed our mind that we hadn't arranged for a pick up as the speed-boat disappeared back around the headland.

We had landed on the uninhabited side of the island and set up our tent in the lee of a stone wall, not far from the ruins of what is said to have been an all-female Incan monastery. It was the most perfect spot to watch one of the greatest shows on earth, the sun setting over Lake Titicaca. We sat on the wall running across the island's spine, passed the bottle of wine between us and watched the wind scurry cat claws across a vast ellipse of ever deepening purples.

And then the sun dipped behind the horizon and in true Altiplano style the temperature nose dived within the space of a couple of minutes. The wind suddenly switched from benign to perishing and we retreated to the relative shelter of our ragged tent. It was so cold in my thread-bare sleeping bag that I barely slept. We emerged the next morning exhausted and hungry with no food or means of getting off the island. Once said to be a penal colony we were starting to feel like the island's prisoners.

Lucky the Isla de al Luna wasn't as abandoned as it had seemed. We found a small hamlet and approached a fisherman on the shore, who was at first bewildered by the appearance of two disorientated gringos. He only spoke Aymara but seemed very welcoming, happy to free the island of its trapped immigrants. He made space on his floor for the night and his wife prepared us a hearty meal of lamb, corn and *charque*.

The next morning he sailed us back to Copacabana in his fishing boat. For centuries communities on the shores of lake Titicaca have travelled like this in small crafts built from reeds or timber. The experience is so different without an engine, the wind catching the slack sail and quickening the waves against the gunnel.

Pushing on past the last house on the outskirts of Yamani I finally found myself standing alone at the start of the Sacred Route of the Incas. Curling boldly out of Yamani and around the first hill of stepped terraces, this wide stone path had obviously been laid with serious imperial intent. Incan pilgrims would have walked three or four abreast along the route, many accompanied by musicians and dancers.

Striking out along this ancient way I passed three Aymara women bent over wooden looms, propped up with stones. They ran their shuttles through a dense weave of fibres with worn, dextrous fingers. Beyond, a boy shepherd drove a clutch of sheep ahead of him with a handful of small, well-directed pebbles. So little had changed.

The Incas planted trees to break up the island's open monotony. Patches of woodland remain, offering dappled shade and a whispered sense of movement in the breeze. The rhythm of my stride echoed the terraces' graceful contours, the lake a glassy mirror to my thoughts.

I wondered if Dad ever made it to the *Isla Del Sol* during his time in the Altiplano. Although he never mentioned the island, he talked often about Lake Titicaca. I thought it unlikely that he would have missed this walk and sensed his footfall by my side. For a moment we were kicking up the same heat and dust on this song line across the island. Our shadows merging under the sun's relentless glare.

Out of the trees the route climbed sharply to the island's highest point, a rocky outcrop beyond which the rest of the island lay hidden from view. Devoid of any shade, this long, high altitude climb was enough to break down the hardiest of pilgrims. Head bowed, gulping for breath, my eyes followed the fissured lattice of rock that ran under my feet as I walked up the slope. My vision blurred, the red sandstone looked more like densely packed veins, giving way to chalky, bone bleached fingers pushing up from below. The patterns slowed and ebbed. I steadied myself on a large stone, moulded perfectly by a million weary backsides, and fought for oxygen.

A beetle gradually crawled past my foot, pushing forward a perfectly formed pellet of dung on its lonely path to the summit. 'Christ,' said the pounding blood in my head, 'this is like some dreadful scene from *Pilgrim's Progress*.' 'Quick, you've got to stand up and beat that beetle to the top before you fall into the slough of despond,' I told myself. Then it occurred to me that the beetle and I were, in fact, old companions. We had both been pushing shit uphill for most of our lives.

When I hit my teenage years my feelings of abandonment by Dad shifted into trackless rage. I vented my fury on everyone around me, particularly those who I loved the most. My younger brother spent many of these years virtually barricaded in his bedroom. I once actually smashed through his door with a narwhal's tusk, another of dad's obscure heirlooms from his travels. Mum, at her wits' end, confiscated the tusk and threw it away.

There was little more she could do to contain the fallout in her nuclear family. I can still picture her crying on the stairs of our terraced house as I stormed out in one of my rages, telling her to 'piss off and get the f*** out of my life.' By the time I hit seventeen I was so toxic that she moved me into the basement with my own, separate entrance around the back.

I reserved much of my destructive spirit for myself, limping through school only to spectacularly fail my A levels. I remember phoning Dad up in Brazil, eager to break the news, to get a rise. I told him that I had been awarded an E, an F and a U for Un-Classified (which I still consider an achievement of sorts).

'I'll bet you are proud of me now,' I said, my voice trembling. His muffled reply was so elegantly weighted across the thousands of miles of static and ocean: 'I'll always be proud of you, whatever you do.' Those words only inflamed me further. I wanted a parent, angry and involved in my life – not the measured indifference of a priest.

A pair of sandaled feet shuffled into my narrow field of view. Looking up they connected to a small middle-aged Aymara man with skin like beaten leather and two remaining front teeth, set apart at jaunty angles. Beaming at me ear to ear, he offered up a handful of coca leaves.

Coca may have been demonised in the West as the principle ingredient in cocaine, but in the Altiplano it remains deeply rooted in the popular imagination of the people who have cultivated and used it for centuries. Much more than a source of nutrition and relief from altitude sickness, it is also an essential conduit for communications in both the visible and spirit worlds.

As I stripped each leaf to the spine with my front teeth and pushed them into the side of my cheek, my companion told me the name of every surrounding hill in Quechua, the language of the Incas. Their order was lost to me but the cadence of his speech rose and fell with the island's undulating symmetry.

'*Mira*', he said pointing excitedly into the sky, '*Aguilas*'. Sure enough two big birds of prey circled high in the sky above us. 'This is a good blessing,' he told me. 'The eagles mean good luck in your journey, they give energy.' I thought of Thor and his two ravens, one representing memory and the other thought. A moment later and my messenger, together with his two eagles, had gone. I watched him speed-walk over the hill in a cocked hat and a brilliant blue jumper.

The summit brought with it an immense sense of relief. From here the route traced the island's ridges across a series of switch back peaks into the far north of the island. Knowing that the hardest section was past, I quickened my step across the roof of the world.

It is hard to imagine just how the early pilgrims must have felt as they walked these last few miles to the sacred rock, which is said to resemble the head of a puma. To them this place was the source of all creation. According to an account in the 17th century by the Jesuit priest Bernabé Cobo the island's high priests stage-managed expectations with a series of purification rituals along the way. Only those deemed to have a clean enough conscience, together with suitably high social standing, were allowed to complete their journey. The rest were siphoned off to a separate area where they could watch the ceremonies from afar.

Nowadays the centrepiece of all their intent is easily overlooked. I dropped down from high rocky ground to a small green plateau next to a large, sandstone outcrop. Rain and wind have sculptured the soft, russet stone into a honeycomb of natural alcoves. Beyond, the remains of the Incan temple of Chincana sprawled down a steep slope, towards the wide arc of a sandy beach below.

A teenage girl appeared out of nowhere to tell me that this weathered sandstone protrusion was indeed the fabled sacred rock. We were standing in the '*santuario*,' where priests performed elaborate ceremonies to mark key moments in the astrological calendar, such as the summer and winter solstices. She pointed out a collection of naturally eroded lines in the stone that are said to represent the face of Inti, the God of the Sun, being kissed on the cheek by Mama Quilla, the Goddess of the Moon.

'Legend has it that Mama Quilla chased Inti out of this rock and has been hotly pursuing him across the sky ever since,' my self-appointed guide told me in a listless monotone, perfected from endless repetition. I gave her a few coins and wandered off to find some shade amongst the faded symbols of another people's religion. I may have felt some empathy for the island's ghostly pilgrims on their route across the island, but this place left me oddly cold.

Waiting in the shade of a large boulder for the sun's brilliant gaze to cool and dip towards the horizon I had a vivid memory of one of the few times that I met up with my father when I was a young man. He had arranged to meet my brother and me at an exclusive French restaurant on one of his infrequent business trips to London. By this stage in his life he was a senior manager in exploration and had long since swapped his field kit and rations for tailored Italian suits and a taste for fine cuisine.

As soon as the over-attentive waiters had seated us and spirited away our jackets, Dad made a graceful lunge for the wine menu. He was long sighted and had to hold it out at arm's length, to both read and effectively shield himself from the two deeply troubled adolescents sitting opposite him.

A twitch of an eyebrow summoned the waiter – Dad had a formidable authority with restaurant staff – and the first of several bottles of flinty Chablis was poured into our glasses. He maintained formal radio silence until the first bottle had been sunk, punctuating his towering reserve with the occasional hmm, or 'well, yes.' All the while I wanted to shout at him, shake him, rip the whole place up.

Half way through the second bottle and he was ready to push away from the handrail, like a novice ice skater, into some conversation. We stuck to neutral ground: British politics, the parlous state of the copper market, deforestation in the Amazon. As soon as my brother or I dared stray into anything personal, Dad clammed up and the silence floated back in to envelop us again like an East Coast haar. I remember wishing that I could have asked one of the waiters to discreetly cordon off our table with police accident tape.

After coffee, Dad ordered the single malts. Suitably lubricated, he tried out some 'fatherly advice.' His tired phrases, such as 'you do realise that there will be no free lunches from now on,' fell on deaf ears. The only comment that stuck me as genuine must have been drawn from his own experience of trading an outdoor life for office work. 'Whatever you do,' he warned us, 'don't end up in a desk job.'

Our family reunions invariably ended up with the cheque writing ritual, 'to help with your studies' (by this stage I had been diagnosed dyslexic, passed my re-takes and been accepted for university). It was the part of our meetings that we all dreaded the most. Dad sat watching his inky signature dry on the open chequebook, while my brother and I feigned disinterest. It felt, in that moment, as though our relationship had been distilled to this singular, financial obligation.

It was only as we parted that something slipped. Dad gave us the smile that he usually reserved for the mountains. A joyful grin that radiated warmth and mirth. It disarmed us and left me more understanding of his terrible predicament. We knew that he loved us and that this man of action rather than words desperately wished he could somehow heal the wounds that so tightly bound us.

I'll never forget the time when, as teenagers, we went on a rare winter holiday with him to Northern Portugal. Walking along a deserted beach one stormy afternoon we came across a wide stream running from the mainland into the sea. To save us taking off our shoes Dad piggybacked us, one after the other, to the far side. It was such a tender gesture; carrying his two overgrown sons over the water, trying to somehow lift us clear of our own painful becoming.

Looking past the sacred rock I saw one last summit, dusted white with chalky soil. It was the highest point of the island's most northerly peninsula, a final thrust of land before the lake took hold. Deciding to walk on past the Inca's route, I followed a wavering sheep path onto this last hill.

It wasn't long before the trail petered out. The island's stone terracing gave way to unproductive soil, sprouted with the plump, spiky leaves of yellowing cactus. I realised with a delicious tingle of nervous excitement that I had finally reached somewhere wild. Here, at last, people were no longer trying to interpret the landscape, to bend it to their own religious and political purpose.

I sat on the headland looking over a small cove. From this view point the lake expanded outwards towards a broken rim of jagged peaks, topped with a high banner of cirrus cloud. The immaculate sky seemed stretched thin by the late afternoon's marbled glaze.

I watched currents snake across the lake's surface, like great brush strokes on a taut blue canvas, and felt something give inside of me. Silence and then a fragment of Seamus Heaney: *And after the commanded journey, what? Nothing magnificent, nothing unknown. A gazing out from far away, alone.*

After Dad died there was something that I didn't admit to anyone. It wasn't overwhelming grief and sadness that I felt from his loss, but rage. The old bear came back, haunting me at night and when I walked alone. How could he drop-out like that without any warning, just disappear from one day to the next without giving me even a chance to get to know him? It was like a final insult, abandoning me to spend the rest of my life shadow boxing with a stranger.

I realised that it is this angry boy seeking reproach that had driven me back out to Bolivia, demanding some 'final reckoning' with my father. Only now did I finally see that the true purpose of my journey was to say goodbye, to finally let go. To love the man he was, rather than hate the father he wasn't. I had come seeking answers and somehow found my way back to forgiveness.

A storm had begun gathering along the brooding rim of mountains, for once humbled by black cloud and bright water. The wind rose sharply at my back, tugged at the cuffs of my jacket, calling me urgently back: 'Only one life,' it whispered, 'one moment, one chance.'

YUNGAS CRUZ

'Are you ready for four days of adventure?' my guide Sixto asked with a big grin as we unloaded our camping gear out of the back of a taxi. We stood together at the edge of the handful of adobe houses and peered beyond a scattering of plastic bottles into the void of swirling mist and rain. I could just about make out a narrow path, smudged like ink on blotting paper as it wound out onto a barren rise of rocky ground.

And then the cloud shifted to reveal a flash of emerald mountains, tumbling away below us towards the Amazon basin somewhere far, far beyond. Caught unawares, a rush of vertigo rippled through me. I blinked and it was all swept away again – the Yungas Cruz wasn't about to give itself up lightly.

Walking across the spine of the Island of the Sun had been an intense experience and I'd loved the sense of connection it brought to a deeper past. But the 7km route wasn't much of a physical challenge. I was hungry for more and there was nothing more enticing than tracing an ancient trade route from the high plains into the steppes of the Andes.

The Yungas Cruz is one of a sophisticated network of pre-Columbian paths that were built between the Altiplano and the fertile valleys below. In parts they are highways of paved stone, engineered to carry huge llama caravans laden with produce. These trade arteries were once essential to the flow of fruit, vegetables and coca leaves from the Yungas region to the people of the high plains.

Although the bulk of this commerce has long shifted to the roads, a few of these routes have been kept open. Well known Bolivian trails such as the Takesi, the Yungas Cruz and the Choro are still used to transport minerals, tools, food, cattle and contraband between scattered communities. Walking one of these slender links to the outside world seemed the best way to leave the Altiplano region, together with my past, behind.

Out of all of these trails the Yungas Cruz most appealed to my sense of adventure. Thought to long pre-date the Incan empire, much of its original stonework has been eroded by weather and time. The tenuous path that remains is barely kept open by the farmers who use it occasionally to drive their cattle to Chulumani for market. When I told Lindsay that I planned to walk it he just whistled through his teeth and advised me to take a guide, a shotgun and to 'be prepared for every eventuality.'

Luckily my guide had come well equipped. Together with tents, sleeping bags and a huge cast iron camping stove, we unloaded two machetes, first aid supplies, climbing rope, a spade and what looked like several fireworks out of the taxi (I wonder just what it was that he was planning to celebrate). There were also three large black garbage bags bulging with frankfurters, bread, rice, apples, bananas and endless jars of coffee and condiments.

By the time Sixto has wrapped it all up in blue plastic sheeting I figured he planned to hire a donkey to get us and all our gear off the mountain. Instead he hauled the whole unwieldy package onto his own back, his slight body doubled-over under its weight. I watched him stabilise himself with a complex system of ropes – meeting in a single knot around his waist – and marvelled at how the Aymara seemed to draw immense strength and stamina from unseen reserves.

Originally from Sajama on the border with Chile, Sixto had over twenty years experience as a porter, cook and guide on high altitude expeditions. In his late 40s, his face was criss-crossed by the sunlight and wind. And yet his open smile still brimmed with youthful enthusiasm. The mountains had kept him happy.

We set a relaxed pace along the trail, tracking the ridges' forward arc through the mist. Before long a towering buttress of black, wet rock leaned out of the gloom. At its base the path shifted from the temporary wear of passing feet, to the hard cut of deliberately worked stone. Here Sixto turned to me and said: 'Welcome to the mountain of San Pedro, a place of rain. From here there is a small ascent.' Looking at the towering rock above us I figured that if this was Sixto's idea of small ascent I was lucky to have missed the long one.

We climbed for hours up a roughly hewn staircase, edging between successive, rugged crags. It was like being trapped at the centre of a silent planet of grey cloud. Fine tendrils of mist looped in towards us like coiled serpents and the silence pressed in so hard on my rasping breath that I felt like a diver, swimming up, frantic for air.

We finally broke out by a small cairn of loose stones that looked straight onto Illimani, laced with snow and blessed by the evening's metallic sunlight. Next to

Illimani, Murata's ragged mouth of broken crowns serrated the sky. For all the times that Sixto had touched such dizzy heights he seemed as moved as I was by the Andes' raw drama. 'Enjoy it while you can,' he said cryptically. 'For this is like a dream, tomorrow it will have all gone.'

The stone that I had picked up along the way fitted snugly into the curve of my hand and was the colour of midnight. When I placed it on the cairn Sixto nodded in approval and told me: 'We call these *apachetas*; high places where travellers leave behind their sorrows.' I thought of my dad and felt the sharp incision of pain that I had carried around like a love letter, or precious bird inside my coat, for so long. Here, if anywhere, felt like a good place to throw this sorrow to the wind.

Music was my father's ultimate solace. He loved classical and J S Bach was by far his favourite composer. At School in Gordonstoun in the 1950s, part of his curriculum was to lie on his back with his year in the sports hall every week and listen to classical music, including Bach's 'musical offering.' The austerity and tangled hierarchy of Bach's piano fugues fascinated and haunted him for the rest of his life. Their playful dance between different voices, all moving away from, echoing or returning to the same principle theme, were his riddle in the sands, a closed intellectual loop without beginning or end.

I remember Dad reverently preparing a vinyl album of Bach's Preludes and Fugues Nos 1 to 12 in his living room one evening when I was a teenager. He slid the record like an ancient scroll out of the paper liner, careful to finely balance it between his index finger and thumb so as not to leave a greasy print on the grooves. He would spend a frustrating amount of time with the record cleaner, which looked much like an old black board rubber. I remember him pressing it endlessly onto the vinyl, as it turned on the table, picking up as much static as dust.

And then the final moment of anticipation. His nose dipped low towards the turntable he gently swung the rocker arm into position, before delicately lowering the stylus onto the record's outer edge. A touch down of crackle and hiss and the speakers spluttered into muted voice. First silence, thick and expectant. And then the piano's melodic notes cut the air with such clarity we could almost feel the air around us expanding. We sat in silence, my dad now back in the sofa with his eyes closed, travelling.

I remember feeling a bit awkward at first, like a drunk turning up to a midnight mass. I couldn't begin to decipher the inner workings of this intricately complex music that drew Dad so deep into its inner chambers. But as I listened the music changed and became breathtakingly beautiful to me. It grew and flowed between us forming a shining bridge, a longship on silver waves. It carried us together, far beyond the standing lamp, the bowl of fruit and the dusking window. I put the same Fugues on my phone as we walked away from the cairn. It still catches at my heart so.

The last light had almost bled from the sky by the time we reached *Kala Cuidad*, the stone city. Here we pitched our tents on a narrow strip of level ground by a burn and crouched around the stove for a quick mug of powdered soup. There was nothing remarkable about the place, a saddle of steep ground between high peaks. But the wind whistling through the rocky moraine of mottled boulders above us unsettled me.

I wasn't the only one on edge. Sixto kept swinging his feeble head torch around the gathering darkness, as though trying to pinpoint some invisible threat. At first I thought it was the pumas that stalk high ground like this that seemed to be making him nervous. 'They will be up there in the city of stones watching us,' he said as he lit a handful of grass and fanned a thin plume of smoke into the wind.' Three shadows flitted overhead. 'Black Ibis,' he told me with an involuntary shudder, 'The Aymara believe they are witches, this is a bad omen.'

He then admitted that it was humans, rather than wild animals, that he feared the most. The two miners that we had passed earlier in the afternoon had seemed innocuous enough to me. Dressed in tracksuit bottoms, trainers and pullovers, they carried nothing more threatening than a transistor radio churning out a faint mix of *cumbia* and static. We had also heard the deep rumble of dynamite in the day and had seen a couple of camps – fragile structures covered in orange plastic sheeting – in the valley beneath us. They were recently opened gold mines, suddenly a lucrative prospect following a price hike on the international markets.

A miner himself in his youth, Sixto warned me that these men could not be trusted in such a remote area. 'Most of them are good people, we are all human beings,' he said. 'But you know they all drink in the mine and some of them, especially the young, have no conscience.' He told me that several tourists had been robbed by miners on the Takesi trail the previous year.

I immediately regretted asking him about the Yungas Cruz. 'Years ago a Dutch couple disappeared here, they never found the bodies,' he told me. The wind rose to a thin wail through the stones above. 'The robbers were jailed after being caught red-handed with the gringos' passports, but bribed their way to freedom six months later,' he added, before disappearing into his tent. I sat up for as long as I could manage in the intense cold, listening to Sixto's contented snoring while clutching my tiny Swiss army knife in the forlorn hope that it might protect us from imminent attack.

It was jackals, rather than miners in hard hats with leering smiles, that woke me the following dawn. At least that is what Sixto called the animals making single high-pitched yaps no more than a hundred metres away in the mist. Having already met one mountain dog (Merlin), I hoped that the barks actually belong to the more diminutive Andean fox. We quickly broke camp and pushed on, heading for a point of sudden descent into the expectant forest below.

All along the main trade routes through the Andes the Incas built rest stops, called *tambos*. These were often large compounds for travellers and their llamas. The surrounding communities were responsible for maintaining them, providing messenger runners to relay news up and down the routes. Many of the *tambos* were maintained throughout the colonial period, when the coca leaf became the dominant trade between the Yungas and Potosi.

We reached the remains of one of these *tambos* in the afternoon, the broken down walls of two large houses, built on a high vantage point above the forest line. There was something about the setting that was eerily familiar to my native Scotland. Deep mosses softened my step underfoot and lichens clung to the branches of a few spindly trees. Only the bird-calls were unfamiliar; a constant peewee, like an inverted wolf whistle, dulled into flat tones by the mist.

The ruins themselves held the same sense of desolate abandonment as the shielings that I had walked to in remote highland glens. The memory of a people somehow distilled into dry stone walls, a cold hearth and fallen lintel. It made for a strange comparison; two distant cultures, such a similar fate.

The first hint that we were descending into the cloud forest was the sound of the wind. It had whipped around us all day with nothing to purchase on. Now it rolled contentedly through the tree-tops in a multitude of hushed voices. The entrance, a narrow break in the dense wall of foliage, looked like a portal to a forbidden world. Before stepping inside Sixto paused, winked and said 'this is where the adventure really starts.'

Three paces later and we were standing within a damp, hushed sanctuary. The trees, no more than five metres high at this altitude, were green with moss and hung with rare orchids and arboreal ferns. They grew at all angles, their slim branches like the tangled limbs of a single entity. Sixto immediately started pointing out the life that crawled, slithered or crept along the forest floor. A black and purple caterpillar with yellow antennae; a thin line of large, black ants with gaping mandibles; a small green snake asleep on the path.

We walked for half an hour, stopping once to inspect a leafy cactus that had been pulled apart at the base to get to its most tender stalks. 'A bear has eaten this within the last hour,' said Sixto. Registering my alarm, he quickly assured me that there was no need to worry. He described the local bears, called *jakumari*, as being black with white noses, vegetarian and no larger than a dog.

Breaking into a clearing in the forest, Sixto dropped his gear and started gathering firewood. No sooner had we put up our tents, started a small fire and settled down for a bowl of soup, then it started. A deep, rumbling roar emanated from the forest above us. We both froze mid slurp, our food forgotten. If the beast that made this noise really was the size of a dachshund, it had a very impressive set of lungs.

'It's a *jakumari*,' Sixto shakily informed me, his early bravado gone. The bear was quickly answered by another below and a third in the undergrowth close to our tents. It sounded like we are surrounded by a pride of hungry lions. Sixto scuttled into his tent to emerge gripping a firework in one hand and a lighter in the other, his last line of defence against wild animals.

'In all my years of guiding I've never heard anything like it,' he whispered. 'What do you think we should do? Let off one of these? I only have three,' Another terrible roar pierced the night, accompanied by the sound of something heavy crashing through the forest close to us. 'What in Christ's name are you asking me for?' I wanted to know, 'you're the one who is supposed to be the guide.'

Worried that fireworks might only enrage the bears further we decided to err on the side of non-intervention. Huddling instead around a stuttering flame like miserable cave men, we frantically tried to coax the damp wood into a respectable deterrent. In desperation Sixto jettisoned the rest of the cooking fuel onto the embers, creating a brilliant, but all too fleeting, bonfire of flame and light.

We took to our tents late into the night once the bear rumpus had quietened down. I felt even more exposed in my sleeping bag, convinced that they would come for me in my sleep. And then I remembered the three Snickers bars in the tent's internal pocket. Don't bears love chocolate? Surely they will sniff it out. What should I do with them? Bury them? Eat them?

A slippery idea eased its way into my head. I could creep out, stash the Snickers under the flysheet of Sixto's tent and make a quick get-away while the bears devoured the expedition guide. Self-preservation is the most ruthless of instincts. In the end I pushed the chocolate into the bottom of my boots and stuffed my now crispy walking socks over the top of them. Nothing, I was certain, would cut through that pong.

Our last day of walking the Yungas Cruz was a blur, a race to reach the valley floor before we ran out of water and light. It was tough going, our progress hampered by the state of the path. In places thousands of years of footfall and rain had furrowed a deep holloway into the bedrock, with banks reaching high above our heads. In others the trail almost disappeared completely, grown over by branches and creeping vines. Sixto had to constantly hack away with his machete, the forest animals melting away ahead to his blade's metallic ring.

Descent, descent, descent. It felt as though we were being rolled off the mountain like a couple of loose stones, yielding helplessly to the irresistible pull of gravity. Sixto must have set the pace deliberately, a relentless momentum that pushed us past stretches of mortal danger before I had time to hesitate. At one point we traversed a sheer cliff face with only a wisp of cloud between us and an almost seductive plunge into thin air. I picked my way along the skinny path, hewn by invisible hands into the rock face, with life and death finely weighted in each step.

When we finally emerged from the forest onto a spit of bare land overlooking the valley basin I was torn between relief and regret. Relief that I had made it and sadness that the Yungas Cruz has come so abruptly to an end. Below us a patchwork of coca fields fanned out with a distinctive, stepped terracing. I could just make out the bent backs of women, picking the spring harvest. At an altitude of 1,700 metres these slopes combine the green fertility of the Amazon in the lowlands with the cooling breezes and open horizons of the high Andes.

The town of Chulumani glittered on an undulating rise across the valley. Although grandly named 'the capital of the southern Yungas,' it looked tiny against the great swathes of evening shadow that were gathered in the Andes' soft folds.

We dropped down to an empty school, stopping in a scrappy yard inhabited by undernourished chickens. A single bulb hung from the crook of a tree and a tap attached to a concrete pillar dripped out a steady beat. Civilisation of sorts.

Night fell, a sickle moon flying over a starless sky. Sixto and I lay exhausted on a pile of wood chips, intoxicated by the warmth and humidity of these lower slopes. Fireflies danced through the bush at the edge of the yard and a cicada burst into evening song.

A villager wandered past as we cooked up powdered mash with frankfurters on an improvised fire of dried cow dung. Sixto asked him about the bears in the now distant forest. 'As big as a small horse' the man replied, with a grand swing of his arms. 'Next time you go, don't forget to take a shotgun.'

Our last night together on the hill, we cracked into the local mountain brew. Drunk across the Altiplano, *té con té* is a euphemism for tea with whatever is alcoholic and to hand. We boiled up a saucepan brimming with water, stewed teabags and *singani*, Bolivia's national grape spirit. The burning elixir, with the kick of a donkey, quickly had us in stitches as we recounted our narrow escape from Sixto's 'pigmy' bears.

Sixto later dropped his voice to tell me of the sorrows that still burdened his heart. He spoke of his father, who died in his arms of cancer only a year earlier. He was a kind man of few words who had tilled the same patch of ground his whole life and could turn anything to use with his hands.

Sixto described how his father would painstakingly cure and cut hide into long strips, before twisting them into a strong, elastic rope to drag the plough behind his oxen. His father clearly lived his entire life with this steady determination and perseverance.

I told him about my father and how his death had drawn me back to Bolivia. We agreed that our fathers sounded like such similar men. Both only spoke when they had something to say. My dad approached everything with the same steadfast diligence. Although worlds apart both men were quiet masters of their fields.

I realised that death had worked its tremendous, transformative power on both of us. We had entered the forest strangers and emerged united by adventure and loss. By the end of the evening I had sworn that Sixto would walk with me one day in the Cairngorms and he had invited me to have dinner with his family back in La Paz.

But first I had a rumour to track down and finally lay to rest in the town of Chulumani, only a few kilometres from where we were camped. It was the ragged edge of a story that had been playing on my mind for many years: A secret history of Nazis, cocaine and murder in paradise.

CHULUMANI

By the time I hobbled into Chulumani, my body in pieces after the rigours of walking the Yungas Cruz in three days rather than the usual five, the town's weekly market was in full swing. The leafy central plaza, surrounded by a network of narrow cobblestoned streets, was buzzing with activity. Children queued for ice cream and congregated in dark rooms flickering with the neon beat of video games. A man dressed in a crisp white shirt and a trilby staggered out of a karaoke bar crying into a jar of beer. It looked set to be a long afternoon.

Farmers from the outlying areas had commandeered every available truck, car and taxi to disgorge brilliant profusions of orange, yellow and red mangos. In a matter of weeks the mango season would pass and attention switch to oranges. I had been told that the oranges were so plentiful that when they ripened they ended up carpeting the roads and the buses would drive into town trailing clouds of citrus scented dust.

But it is coca, rather than fruit, that has long been Chulumani's main produce. The storehouses all around town were brimming with big blue, white and orange sacks of the tiny green leaves. Old men leant against the doorframes of these storerooms, their coca swept high in the dusky shadows behind them.

It was a scene that must have been unchanged for centuries. I realised that in the course of my journey through the Altiplano I had unwittingly traced the coca leaf that still plays such an important role in sustaining the miners of Potosi back to its source. This little leaf grown in the Yungas fuelled the Spanish empire's insatiable desire for silver, souls and conquest. Today it still addicts and corrupts, not as a conduit to the silver trade but as the main ingredient to cocaine.

Some of today's coca production in the Yungas is legal, bound for the domestic market to be chewed as a mild stimulant. However a larger amount than anyone is willing to admit to is undoubtedly destined for illicit cocaine factories dotted around the northern Altiplano. Chulumani felt like a town that was used to keeping secrets.

I had first heard the story of an Austrian-styled Nazi Hotel in Chulumani from a woman that I met in La Paz almost ten years earlier. She had claimed that the Hotel Hamburgo at the edge of town was a meeting place for Nazi war criminals on the run during the late 1940s and early 1950s.

Guests apparently toasted a portrait of the Fuhrer above the mantlepiece, before being served dinner with swastika embossed cutlery. Once the plates had been cleared away they would sing rousing marching songs to the gramophone. At some point in the mid-fifties the Austrian styled building at the edge of town was supposedly pulled down, its bricks spread like the ash from a fire across derelict ground.

When I heard this colourful description of the Hotel Hamburgo I thought it too fantastical to take seriously.

It sounded more like a fictional scene from Frederick Forsyth's *The Odessa File* – the tale of a secretive Nazi network that spirited war criminals out of Europe.

A couple of years later while travelling in Uruguay I spotted an SS officer's cap, complete with the death head insignia, for sale in a flea market in Montevideo. Its dark felt smelt of musty hair and something indistinguishable. Does evil have a smell? Repulsed and fascinated by it at the same time, the experience jogged my memory. Perhaps the story of the Hamburgo wasn't beyond the bounds of possibility after all.

There was a well-organised exodus of thousands of German SS officers and Nazi collaborators to South America after the Second World War. Smuggled into exile along clandestine 'rat lines,' often with the help of Roman Catholic priests, they sailed to the New World with their new identities on fraudulently obtained Red Cross passports. Their flight has been described as 'the greatest escape ever in the annals of crime.'

A few of the most notorious Nazis were eventually tracked down. Mossad agents kidnapped Adolf Eichmann, the supreme commander of the 'Final Solution,' outside his Buenos Aires home in 1960. He was smuggled back to Israel, heavily sedated on an El Al flight, where he was tried and hanged for his crimes against humanity in 1962.

Many Nazi fugitives received life long protection from the right-wing dictatorships that took hold across South America. Josef Mengele, Auschwitz's 'Angel of Death', lived in Argentina, Paraguay and Brazil after the war. He died a free man, drowning off a beach near São Paulo in 1979.

Bolivia's most infamous Nazi resident was Klaus Barbie, also known as the Butcher of Lyon. The Gestapo

Chief in France's third largest city of Lyon, Barbie was responsible for the death of thousands of Jews and French resistance fighters during the war. Described as a man of 'brutal instinct,' it was Barbie who captured and murdered the head of the French Resistance, Jean Moulin, in 1943.

Barbie fled to Bolivia with his family in 1951. Despite being condemned to death by two military tribunals in France he was a regular sight in La Paz for the next thirty years, posing as a genial businessman in a sports jacket, tie and Tyrolean hat. His favourite haunt was the Confiteria Club de La Paz on Calle Camacho. The gathering place for Bolivia's political elite, the café was often called Bolivia's 'parallel parliament' for it's febrile atmosphere of plotting and intrigue.

I used to visit the café when I lived in La Paz. Back then it was one of the few places in the city where you could get a half decent coffee (rather than the thick syrup topped up with warm water that was then typical of most Bolivian establishments). Wood-lined and thick with cigarette smoke, it remained virtually unchanged from the time when Barbie was a regular. Waitresses still made their long sorties with tall glasses of juice, apple cake and hot drinks to small groups of sharply dressed elderly men, deep in hushed conversation. Barbie would often sit apart with his regular cup of black coffee.

It was the perfect place for him to orchestrate his murky dealings in South America's 'dirty war' against communism. Barbie traded, sold, and invented information on left wing unions, students and political groups for a string of right wing military dictatorships. He even boasted that he played a part in Che Guevara's capture and death in Bolivia in 1967.

The more indispensable Barbie made himself to Bolivia's dictators, the more powerful and untouchable he became. He trafficked arms to similar regimes in South America through a network of Nazi contacts and built up a small army of mercenaries to protect the cocaine trade in the east of the country.

At the height of his influence, during General Garcia Mesa's bloody coup in 1980, Barbie's squads of mercenaries (nicknamed the Fiancés of Death) terrorised La Paz's streets while Barbie himself toured the prisons advising on torture techniques. His efforts were even rewarded with the honorary title of Lieutenant Colonel in the Bolivian army during Mesa's short-lived regime.

Barbie's immunity from his past crumbled with Bolivia's return to democracy in 1982. President Siles Zuarez had him bundled into a military transport plane and flown to Europe to be tried for his crimes against humanity. Once in France he was escorted back through the imposing entrance to the Montluc prison fortress in Lyon where he had committed his worst crimes forty years earlier. For Barbie history came full circle. He was sentenced to life imprisonment and died in custody of leukaemia in 1991.

I wandered out of the bustling town centre to the area of rough ground where I had been told the Hotel Hamburgo once stood. All I had to go on was a description of the long demolished hotel with its wide veranda and swimming pool. At first my search only confirmed my doubts. There was no sign of the foundations of a building as large, or as well built, as the one that had been described to me.

And then, half covered by a tangle of wild flowers and vines, I stumbled across the crumbling remains of an Olympic scaled swimming pool. A knot of fear tightened in my stomach as I stared into its' concrete depths. Who would have the money or inclination to build such a large swimming pool so long ago and so far from anywhere? Suddenly the bizarre tale of the Hamburgo seemed closer, more tangible. It felt like I had just plunged my hand deep in a dark hole and touched something cold and wet, recoiling from my fingertips.

Could the Hotel Hamburgo have once been what the Nazi hunter Simon Wiesenthal described as an *Anlaufstelle* (harbour area) in the ODESSA network? In Europe these were often inns in secluded, forested areas that provided refuge for Nazi criminals on the run. Chulumani in the 1940s was a one-horse town surrounded by a vast, semi-tropical jungle. It was only connected to La Paz by a mountain road that even today remains impassable in heavy rain. There must have been few places as remote from the Nuremburg Trials in Europe as this one.

I tried to imagine the men and women sunbathing around the pool, their bronzed bodies relaxing under the tropical sun. In my mind's eye they drank cocktails in Panama hats and swam neat lengths through clear water, so far from the horrors back home. They talked excitedly about plans for their new lives in exile as well as discussing how their *Kameradenwerk* would crush the communist threat in South America.

Some were even more ambitious, predicting the rise of a Fourth Reich across the world from the ashes of defeat. Their war would only end when they passed away, their graves marked with assumed names. Most would live out the rest of their natural lives free from justice, never to be punished for their crimes.

South America became a safe haven for many of the victims of the Nazis as well. I had once met up with a Basque anarchist in the Bolivian Amazon who had fought Franco in the Spanish Civil War before joining the French army to try and halt Hitler's march across Western Europe. Captured by German infantry he told me that he had survived three years as a political prisoner of war in Belsen. He even claimed that Heinrich Himmler once came to visit him in person because he had gained celebrity status for being the prisoner that just wouldn't die.

After the horrors of the war the Basque had decided to turn his back for ever on European 'civilisation,' finding solace in the remote Beni region of the Bolivian jungle back in the 1950s. Half crazed by tropical heat and isolation, he had clearly kept himself busy in his jungle retreat with three local indigenous wives and a gaggle of children. He named the village that he had founded and populated single handedly the *Independent Anarchist Repububblic of Quiquibey* (IARQ). True to his political principles there were no rules in his dominion, other than a total ban on the circulation of currency. When I met the Basque he was a very old man but still strong and lucid. There was no way of corroborating his story, other than the faded serial number tattooed on his forearm from his time in Belsen.

Admittedly an abandoned swimming pool in some waste ground on the outskirts of Chulumani wasn't much of a discovery, but it propelled me on. If some of the shadowy individuals who stayed in the Hamburgo settled in the area, I figured that they were most likely to be buried in the town's graveyard. Perhaps the names on the headstones would offer up some further clues.

Chulumani's cemetery was a rambling enclosure of steep land fifteen minutes' walk from town. As I entered a group of resident weaver birds with brilliant yellow tails flited from long nests of dry grasses, hung in the tall trees overhead. They seemed like restless spirits, keeping a constant vigil over the graveyard's ramshackle collection of lopsided headstones.

Most of the lettering on these stones was overgrown, or worn away. I found a few Jewish names, each marked with a Star of David. In a final insult to their victims some Nazis took on Jewish names after the war to conceal their true identities. There were also a couple of Germans buried in the cemetery, but this was hardly proof of a Nazi presence in Chulumani. There has been a small, influential German community in Bolivia since the 1920s.

I was about to leave when a group of three elderly mourners waved me over. They were sitting on a dilapidated tomb, chatting away merrily to football commentary on a tinny radio. Dressed in shorts, Hawaiian shirts and wide brimmed straw hats, they looked like a small island of colour and good cheer in the gloomy cemetery.

José introduced me to his wife and cousin in an Argentine accent, before handing me a gourd of *yierba mate* with a silver straw. He explained that they all grew up in the town, but had spent most of their working lives in Argentina. Despite living in Buenos Aires, they still came back to Chulumani every year to pay their respects to José's long departed mother.

The family were in the process of repairing the tomb, a decrepit brick construction with its tin roof lying to one side. Earlier that day they had discovered that Jose's mother's remains had disappeared. 'Someone has taken everything,' the cousin said. She leaned forward and whispered, "They use the bones for satanic rituals in the countryside.'

José suddenly jumped up and swept his hand across the loose assortment of bricks. 'All that matters is that this is where my mother was laid to rest over 40 years ago,' he proclaimed. 'She is my Virgin Mary, the woman who bore me for nine months and cared for me when I was a child. She is the woman of my life.' His eyes welled up with tears.

Sensing that the mood was about to plunge into despair, I asked them about the *gringos* that lived in the area fifty years ago. They all jumped at the opportunity to reminisce about their youth in Chulumani, remembering the Hotel Hamburgo as 'a luxury hotel, for foreigners and Bolivian dignitaries only.' José told me that the hotel's owner, Doña Maria, used to strut around the place with a long riding whip and leather boots.

He told me that everyone in the village knew that the gringos had escaped from a war in Europe. The first of them were rumoured to have arrived by submarine, washed up on a Uruguayan beach in a rubber dingy one moonless night in 1945. But the Yungas was so far from the rest of the world back then that nobody particularly cared. One of his Bolivian school friends, who worked in the Hotel Hamburgo as a boy, went on to name his sons Hitler and Eichmann Mamani Mamani.

'They were gentlemen, true gentlemen,' Jose reminisced. 'Not all of them,' his sister cut in. 'That Klaus who lived in the corner house down the hill never spoke to anyone. He used to dress like a peasant and come up to the village on a mule to sell his wife's marmalade in the plaza.' When I asked her if she remembered his full name she said she thought his last name was Altmann, but everyone knew him as 'Don Klaus.'

Altmann was the alias that Klaus Barbie arrived under when he first came to Bolivia. It was hard to believe that the same 'Don Klaus' could ever have been in Chulumani selling marmalade, but there are references to him living with his family in the Yungas between 1951 and 1956. He is thought to have worked as a carpenter during this time, keeping a low profile to shake off his pursuers in Europe.

My friends in the cemetery had another intriguing suggestion. They said that Don Klaus had been in league with a mysterious group of Germans who lived in a remote valley of virgin forest called Colaya. 'The rumour was that they were mining gold up there,' one of the women said. She added that Barbie guarded the only road into Colaya, lifting the wooden planks on the bridge in front of his house every evening so that no one could pass through at night.

To get to Colaya they told me to follow a thin dusty road that wound around the entire valley, pass through two villages and follow a track into the hills. Although it sounded like a wild goose chase, the smallest possibility of discovering a long abandoned Nazi hideout in the jungle proved too tempting to resist.

From the cemetery the road to Colaya took me straight past Barbie's house, by a bridge over a small stream that runs out of a wooded gorge. His old home looked more like a military enclosure than a private residence. There was an imposing chain fence, 'Keep Out' signs, and a concrete sentry hut blocks the drive. Beyond I could just make out a low building set back amongst the trees. I felt sickened to think that this notorious war criminal could have enjoyed such comfortable anonymity in the Yungas.

He was remembered for having spent much of his time playing cards with his cronies around his private pool in the grounds. After he was finally arrested the Bolivan army turned up and dug holes all over the garden looking for gold but left empty handed. The cache of Nazi treasure is said to have been hidden under the pool's foundations and spirited away under their noses.

After several hours of tramping under a blazing sun along the deserted road, Colaya began to recede to a mirage in my mind. Hot, thirsty and out of water I dropped into the cool shade of a banana plantation where I spotted a faint trail, headed downhill towards the sound of running water. I hoped this river would lead me on a more direct route to the Germans' long abandoned jungle retreat.

In a clearing by the river I met an old man eating oranges. He was sitting with his back against an adobe hut, a wooden catapult and a handful of stones by his side. Surprisingly unfazed by my sudden appearance, he stood up to welcome me with a broad grin, introducing himself as Fernando. He looked wiry and supple for his years but his face was worn and tight from the sun.

Fernando explained that he came to this orange grove every day in the spring to keep the birds from eating his fruit. He demonstrated with his catapult, flicking a keenly guided pebble high into the canopy of a nearby tree. He said that he had worked the same few acres of land his whole life, ever since it was handed over to his family as part of the agrarian reform that broke up the landed estates following the political revolution of 1952. I realised that the path that had led me straight to this spot had been worn by the singular traffic of Fernando's daily commute.

When I told him that I was heading for Colaya in search of the remains of the Germans that once lived here he wasn't surprised. 'I've been waiting for someone to come back,' he said excitedly. 'You must be one of their relatives.' I explained that I was just a traveller who had heard the stories about the men who lived there and was trying to find out a little more about them. Fernando seemed content with this explanation, inviting me to sit beside him while he peeled and divided his oranges. Judging by how thin he was I guess that this was virtually all he lived on.

Fernando was a boy when a German gringo named Freddie built his 'mansion' in the jungle at the head of the Colaya valley. He described it as a big stone building with a courtyard and a large bread oven in the kitchen. The house had a generator that provided electricity, unheard of in the area at the time, and a radio for Freddie to talk to his friends. A steady flow of German guests, most of them men, came to visit during this time. Some stayed for long periods. Fernando told me that there were several other *gringos* living in smaller houses in the area, but that his memory of them was hazy.

Fernando's father, together with most of the residents in his village, cleared land to grow fruit, coffee and coca for Freddie. The main crop was coca, planted in fields of neat, stone terraces. Only it wasn't just the leaves that they were producing. Fernando described pits filled with alcohol and kerosene where the locals would trample the leaves after each harvest, an essential process in the production of cocaine. 'When we picked the coca it was green, but what they took it out by mule it was white,' he said with a wink.

It didn't take much to persuade Fernando to take a break from his chilled work schedule to show me the ruin of Freddie's old place. I struggled to keep up as he guided me along a fine network of tracks, threading through coffee, citrus and a coca plantations. We passed a small hydro electric scheme and picked up a more pronounced path, sloping gently uphill besides a tumbling river.

Above us, in the misty blue curve between two steeply sided mountains, lay Colaya. Although gradually encroached by coca plantations this remote valley is still a wild and beautiful place. The further we followed the river, the closer the jungle crept in around us. At a small waterfall a profusion of red butterflies danced over the cascading water. When we stopped to drink they alighted on my boots and trousers, their crimson wings swept in rippled unison by the breeze.

Before long Fernando started pointing out signs of a more settled past: A crumbling building with banana trees growing through the open roof; the remnants of a coffee plantation; a curve of stone terracing through tree roots and ferns. Then he stopped at what looked like the stone footprint of a small hut, sunken in the centre with the remains of a drainage channel running through it. This, he told me, was once a rudimentary cocaine factory.

Freddie's house was a little further on, where the banks of the river widened and levelled out. All that was left of the large structure were the stone external walls and an ancient generator, half submerged in water. It would have once been a substantial property with room enough for a big kitchen living area and six or seven bedrooms upstairs.

I stood with Fernando in the tangled debris of rock and leaf litter and tried to imagine this place as a working hacienda. There was no shortage of fertile ground here for crops or livestock. The surrounding jungle would have provided plenty of fruit and game and the nearby river had a limitless supply of fresh water and fish. Freddie and his guests would have easily lived comfortably here unnoticed for the rest of their lives.

And yet for a tiny slice of paradise Colaya felt humid and oppressive. I'm not sure if it was the sense of being hemmed in by a dense tree canopy and the roar of the river, or something more. Perhaps this place still held the collective memory of a band of desperate men, holed up for what must have felt like an eternity in the forest.

After their flight from Europe they would have had a lot of time here to contemplate what they had left behind. They may have escaped their persecutors back home but Colaya didn't seem like a place where you could turn away from your own conscience. I wondered if there was time yet, for some of these individuals, for redemption.

Freddie escaped both. According to Fernando Colaya was abandoned in the mid fifties after Freddie was murdered by one of his own workers. 'They found his body by a pool of fresh water a week after he disappeared,' he said. 'His hipflask had been poisoned by a servant, who fled with his gold.' Fernando swore that he had seen Freddie's gold once in the big house with his own eyes. 'A big jar full of rings and gold crowns,' he added.

I'm not sure if Fernando registered my sharp intake of breath. Much of the Nazi gold was taken from the fingers and teeth of their Jewish victims. One of the biggest known shipments was 250 kilos of gold that was gathered from death camps in Croatia and packed into 12 cases, before being smuggled into South America in 1951.

We stood together for a while in silence. As my head swam with images of jungle fugitives, cocaine smuggling and Nazi gold I felt a chill creep over me. The trees were darkening into silhouettes, the sky touched to a deepening blue. It felt like this secret history was passing out of memory into the dusk around us. Perhaps, I wondered, the secrets in this place of long shadows were better left un-gathered.

My father Nigel in his mother Betty's arms, with his sister
Biddy and brother Simon

Dad, nicknamed Pudge,
catching fish with his sister
Biddy

My father, aged 19, climbing
with a friend

Nigel and Lucy on their
wedding day in Sydney, 1967

My father's early days in
exploration, Papua New Guinea

Papua New Guinea

My arrival, 1970

Mum and Dad with me as a toddler

LEFT: How I remember him, always with his nose in a book

BELOW: Trying so hard to fill his shoes from very young

RIGHT: Flying my stunt kite with Dad in Glenelg

BELOW: I guess my younger brother Charlie should get a look in!

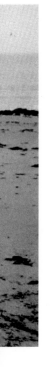

LEFT: Walking with my father in Glenelg

BOTTOM LEFT: My mother, Charlie and me on the West Coast

BELOW: My father in the field

My father in Brazil

SOMEWHERE NEARBY

Macario stepped out of the low adobe house into the dusty courtyard wearing a yellow Brazilian football shirt and an oversized straw cowboy hat. His face was long and drawn but he still looked younger and somehow more normal than I imagined for a witch doctor. He greeted me wordlessly with the disturbing combination of a limp handshake and piercing look, before with a single command putting the two girls at his side to work.

The younger of his daughters stoked the cooking fire in the courtyard while the other busied herself with dinner inside. I was left to sit on a low bench outside, watching orange flames from the fire spit and hiss into the shadows. An assortment of scrawny kittens meowed plaintively for food. It felt weird being drawn so unexpectedly into the intimacy of this family hearth, surrounded by strangers and with little chance of making it back to Chulumani in the dark.

I had walked to the village in the forest to ask Macario if he would hold a *mesa* for me to help lift the shadow of grief that hung over my heart. A *mesa*, the Spanish word for a Christian mass, is the term for a magic ritual in the Andes. The stall holders in the witches' market in La Paz sell the bewildering array of bright charms that make up a *mesa*. Their jumbled mix of beads, incense, clay figures, fresh herbs, llama foetuses and bottles of dubious looking elixirs had always fascinated me. But this was the closest that I had managed to get to the Altiplano's spirit world as the rituals are mostly carried out in private and well away from foreign, prying eyes.

Magic is a much more important part of everyday life than most people in Bolivia would freely admit. Shamans, or *yatiris* as they are known, are most commonly employed as fortune-tellers. They read the coca leaves, much as a tarot reader or astrologer would, to look into someone's past, present and future.

But these fortune tellers have the power to influence events as much as predict them. They are used to ensure the success of a business, to protect a house and family from illness and even to add speed and accuracy to cupid's arrow. There is also a darker side to a *yatiri's* work, using black magic to settle grudges, debts, family feuds and jealousies.

The coca leaf is at the heart of all these rituals. Coca is used as the sacred conduit between the *yatiri* and the conflicting array of spirits, gods, goddesses and saints that populate the Andean mystical world. The coca leaf predicts the future, informs the *yatiri* of the correct course of action to remedy a situation and is used in any offering, spell, or healing charm.

To have the second sight of a *yatiri* you have to be marked out as different. Some are born with physical deformities or birth marks on their face. I had even heard of one man who took up the profession after going bald – hair loss is a rare occurrence in the Andes. I was told that Macario was chosen by a lighting strike that left him with a streak of silver through his raven hair.

By the time he emerged from the kitchen, with a large pan of soup to be boiled up on the fire, darkness had fallen completely and the Andes had shrunk to a circular pool of light around the hearth. He set the pan down on the embers and crouched down beside me to stir the contents.

He sat silently, like a GP in a doctor's surgery back home, while I explained my predicament. I told him how I had been struggling to come to terms with the loss of my father and that this had drawn me away from my own family. I admitted how I felt like I had come to find my Dad's wandering spirit in the high Andes. For an excruciatingly long time he said nothing, seemingly lost in thought as he considered my case.

When he finally spoke in a hushed tone the fire had almost gone out. 'Although I would not normally do this for a gringo I will make an exception for you, provided you buy two cases of beer for next weekend's fiesta,' he told me. I was thrilled that my visit had coincided with a shortage of alcohol for an up coming community event, if a little surprised at such a business-like arrangement. We shook hands on a straight swap of booze for magic.

Macario offered me a bowl of soup made of dried mutton with local vegetables and spaghetti in a tin bowl. Aymara communities butcher and hang the salted sheep on long poles in the Altiplano to desiccate in the drying winds. Curing mutton known as *chalone,* together with dried llama or *charque,* is an ancient Andean technique that has remained the main source of protein for communities such as this one.

It is also another example of the close trading links between the high plains of the Altiplano and the Yungas region. I thought of the Inca llama caravans picking their way through perilous mountain passes that I had recently walked through, carrying coca and fresh fruit to exchange for salt and dried meat. It seemed such a harmonious exchange between interdependent communities from such different ecosystems. The soup, with its rich balance of protein and fresh vegetables was as sustaining as these ancient links.

No sooner had I finished my soup than Macario started diving in and out of the adjacent store room with bulky packages, candles, beer bottles and a small mannequin of a man on horseback. The air seemed charged with a sense of expectation. There is no set pattern to a magic session, a craft which is handed down informally from generation to generation. But there are some ground rules. Most significant of all is the day of the week. Mondays are for honouring your family. Candles are often lit and prayers said for departed loved ones who continue to play an intimate role in daily family life.

Tuesday is dedicated to the spirits of the sky who hold powerful sway over events. This is the day that prisoners use magic to try and influence the outcome of their legal cases. Wednesdays and Thursdays are blank days and are generally an opportunity to have a positive influence in the worlds of work, health, love and financial dealings. Fridays are for your enemies.

The use of black magic is generally frowned upon in the Altiplano, but there is no simple Christian division between good and evil. A good example is the *Pacha Mama*, the earth goddess and symbol of fertility, life and productivity. The *Pacha Mama* is similar to the Virgin Mary in Andean religion and is often called upon with the offering of a splash of alcohol as a benevolent provider of good fortune. But she also plays a central role in more malevolent rituals. It seems the Andean Gods are as fickle and as open to persuasion as their ancient Greek relatives.

I had the feeling that I was entering an uncharted moral universe as I ducked under a low entrance into Macario's house. I half expected to find a pentagram of tea lights on the floor and the soon to be beheaded chickens cowering in the corner. But the bare room was lit by a lone light bulb and had no furniture or strange markings. As we settled down on a circle of blankets for the evening's proceedings Macario reassured me that being a Tuesday he was about to carry out good magic, calling on the spirits of the sky and the saints to protect my home and family.

He kicked off with a long mumbled prayer before lighting two candles in front of a large doll-like mannequin of a Spanish conquistador astride a white horse. The doll had a red cape and was poised with sword held high, about to slay a small red devil tangled under the feet of his horse. 'That is the saint Santiago,' Macario told me. 'He is considered one of the most powerful saints and is also known as the God of Thunder and will be watching over us this evening.'

When the Spanish converted the people of the New World to Catholicism they didn't have time to ask too many questions. Every 'Indian' that took his or her vows and attended mass was another foot soldier in the race to convert these 'noble savages.' So existing belief systems often lingered on, merging with Christian teachings into new, fantastical forms. The Andean Santiago is one of these mercurial creations, a Catholic saint who rides the white lightning on his Andalucian charger.

Macario cut out a large square from a sheet of brown wrapping paper and began to delicately set out the elements of my life. He used the little figurines and pictures that had so fascinated both me and my father in the witches' market in La Paz. They looked like Plasticine toys no bigger than building blocks, only these were made out of sugar and chalk. Each had a simple image moulded into it. There were animals, people, buildings, saints, the sun, moon and stars. A whole universe marked out in miniature.

At the centre were two tiny figures that symbolised Dad and me. Next to us Macario delicately laid down symbols representing my wife, our child and a tiny roof for our home. Around this he built up a confusing array of saints, supporting spirits and totem animals. There were llamas to look over our affairs, butterflies for good luck and condors to protect our home. It felt like I was watching the Andean world slowly unfolding before my eyes.

Macario treated each of these symbolic jigsaw pieces with great reverence. He spoke to them in turn with an inaudible incantation before deciding where to set them down. I felt he was creating a sort of nativity play, a pictorial narrative of my life, into which he sought to draw the aid of powerful supernatural forces. He then overlay this complex picture with llama hair and fat, herbs, powdered incense and silver tinsel.

Macario had set the scene but the catalyst for this synergy of prayer, spectacle and perhaps even magic was coca. We each took turns to hold a coca leaf in our right hand and sprinkle first cactus wine and then white spirit over Macario's elaborate creation. As we did so he asked the saints and the spirits of the surrounding mountains, rivers and animals to heal my wounded heart and guide me back to my family.

The coca leaves were then laid on top of the *mesa* and the paper wrapped around it to form a bulky, aromatic package to be burnt as an offering to the spirits. We then sat opposite each other for several hours, chewing coca and drinking beer from a single glass. 'We are awaiting the midnight hour,' Macario quietly told me, 'when the spirits come to feed on our offering.'

He asked me who does this magic back home. I told him that there was a time when magic was important but now all we have left is some lingering superstitions and a few part-time druids in Wiltshire. But he wouldn't let go, encouraging me to call up some of the most powerful hills in my Highland home.

The hills I am most drawn to are in Glenlyon where I have lived with my family for many years. They have resonant Gaelic names such *Meall Buidhe, Meall Ghaordaidh* and *Meall Nan Tarmachan*. I thought of them and tried to imagine the time when the people who named these mountains revered them in a similar way. But Macario wasn't going to let me off so lightly. He just sat there, waiting for me to play my full part in his ceremony.

So I closed my eyes, called up my favourite spot in Glenlyon: *Choire nan Fraoch* on the shoulder of *Cairn Gorm*. I pictured myself standing in a small circular shieling with the wide sweep of the glacial bowl that the keepers call 'the sanctuary' beyond. This corrie is a natural shelter for hundreds of deer escaping Glenlyon's harsh winter conditions on the high tops.

In the Spring there are beautiful and delicate alpine flowers in the heather but in my imagination it was the heart of winter with everything buried in deep snow. A bitter wind and spindrift blew off the summit and the tips of my fingers were numb from the cold. Far below I could see the burn frozen to a trickle. But somewhere I heard the sound of running water, or was it children's laughter?

The fire outside burned brightly, a fierce blaze under a foreign sky. I stepped outside to watch the package being ceremoniously placed on a makeshift funeral pyre to the sound of distant thunder. As the fire took hold Macario tossed glasses of cane spirit and beer for 'the spirits' into its heart, sending shooting flames high above us. 'The spirits have accepted the offering, we must now leave them to eat,' he told me.

And then he hugged me and told me not to worry. '"It is a good day", he said, "everything has changed". I broke down. I don't know if I was crying out of sadness, or relief from the sense of being freed from so much grief. I felt almost elated, a lightness of spirit. As though something around me had cleared and lifted. Whether or not Macario's magic was genuine alchemy, or just smoke and mirrors, didn't seem to matter anymore to me. The healing power of his prayer and intent seemed enough to penetrate deeper than the dry scriptures of any prescribed religion.

'La hoja es sagrada,' Macario told me as we went back inside. The leaf is sacred. This is a familiar phrase that I had heard many times before, including as the chorus to a popular Bolivian pop song. I have danced to it in a night club in La Paz, put on as a crowd pleaser at the end of the night -'Coca no es cocaina, es una hoja sagrada.' But it hadn't really rung true before this night.

The tradition of growing coca is deeply rooted in Bolivia's Andean slopes. It is also deeply rooted in the popular imagination of the people who have cultivated and used it for centuries. To most people in the Altiplano coca is an essential source of nutrition, a mild stimulant and a means of communication with the visible and spirit worlds.

It is this sacred power invested in the coca leaf by its people that has eluded our understanding in the whole 'war against drugs.' Most indigenous cultures mark out areas of sacred land, whether it is mountains or burial grounds, to worship and respect. Here in the high Andes the plant has taken on this mantle as a symbol of the natural world that sustains us.

I realised that the coca plant is the Altiplano's unbroken connection to the environment and to their pre-Hispanic past. It is a connection that has so far survived conquest, Catholicism and the DEA. Most would agree that it is also increasingly being cultivated and sold for cocaine production in the Yungas. But by lumping the plant in with its destructive chemical derivative we are denying a people its history and its voice. Demonise coca and you demonise its people.

This long night still had a long way to burn. I had hoped that the spirits would be satisfied with their offering and we could turn in for a good night's kip. But once we ducked back inside it quickly became apparent that we were going to see in the dawn in style. Macario reopened the litre of pure cane alcohol he had previously used as an offering and passed it back to me with an air of ceremony and compulsion. One sip and I could feel this 93% proof fire water burn strips off my throat. By the third round I was simultaneously drunk and hung over.

The coca and cigarettes kept me going until around four in the morning when I wrapped myself in a blanket (which I suspected has been peed on by every one of his six children) and keeled over into a corner. I slept fitfully, waking once to hear frantic digging outside. Macario was burying the ashes from the fire before the dawn broke. It was the end of the ceremony, returning the last remnants of the evening's offerings to the earth for protection before they were revealed to the world by the cold day's light.

I woke curled up on a dirt floor in an empty room. Outside I heard a party in full swing, a discordant symphony of blurred voices. I staggered outside rubbing the dust off my crumpled clothes to a drunken cheer. Macario was still in full flow with his neighbours. They ushered me over to the bench outside the kitchen where they were cooking breakfast and seeing in the steely dawn with a hair of the dog. Supplies must be have been low judging by the gloupy pink liquor I was passed. It tasted of cough mixture and reminded me of the sticky dregs of old Tia Maria, Cointreau and Drambuie bottles that I once drained during an all night game of cards back home.

Macario's brusque manner had melted and he greeted me affectionately with a firm embrace. 'It is good to share,' he said with a searching look. 'You won't forget us,' Macario shouted as I walked down the path forever out of their lives to head back to La Paz and ultimately home to Scotland.

CEMETERIO DE LOS MUERTOS

I had never been to a party in a graveyard before. The gates of La Paz's main cemetery were blocked by a crowd of people, gathered with armfuls of flowers, candles and musical instruments. A mariachi band, complete with black and gold wide brimmed sombreros, burst into full song. It felt like I had joined the warm up act for a carnival.

It was in fact the 2nd of November, the climax of the festival of the *Dia de Los Muertos*, the Day of the Dead. In the Andes this is the date when visiting spirits are thought to take leave of their families, friends and loved ones; when the dead are escorted with prayer, candles and noisy celebrations back to the other side.

I squeezed past the band and looked at a large metal map next to a small chapel for the section of the cemetery where I had arranged to meet Maria. The bewildering network of alleyways looked like the street plan for an entire metropolis.

Most of this city's residents were housed in what looked like miniature 1960s apartment blocks of crumbling concrete with row upon row of alcoves, or *niches*. Each mini apartment was home to the occupant's earthly remains, together with a few mementos: faded photos, plastic flowers, Coca Cola bottles, loaves of stale bread.

There were also grand mausoleums, gothic church towers with the busts of long forgotten notables. One, Mr Walter Morales, went so far as to have his tomb overshadowed by a marble statue of 'the Angel of the Apocalypse,' a delicately balanced girl with a slim body, cumbersome wings and leaden feet. For all their grandeur these memorials to the rich shared the same air of mournful neglect as the rest of the cemetery. In death everyone occupies the same ground.

On this day all of the cemetery's residents were being well attended to by their family and friends. Some played pan pipes; others danced and drank illicit spirits from plastic bottles (drinking is illegal in graveyards). Most just sat around with their candles, cigarettes and memories.

At the feet of each of these odd little groups was what appeared to be a pile of pink and white petals and confetti. It was only as I broke out of the narrow alley and climbed onto the wide green packed with mourners that I realised that they were actually paying homage to the skulls of the dead.

The skulls were all shapes and sizes. Some were ancient coffee coloured craniums with gaping jaws. Others looked younger, paler, with their eye sockets stuffed with cotton wool or covered with a pair of reflective aviator glasses. Many had woollen hats on, one read 'Pedrito,' little Peter. I guessed that many of these skulls belonged to the beloved family members who had passed on. Just how they got hold of them didn't bear contemplating.

It wasn't just families that had come here to reacquaint themselves with their nearest and dearest. This was a time for healing from collective as well as personal loss. The families of the fallen soldiers from the Chaco were there to mark Bolivia's disastrous war with Paraguay in the 1930s that ended in 100,000 casualties on both sides and the loss of a significant chunk of territory to the country's southern neighbour. The relatives of the 69 killed in the 2003 protests that led to the downfall of the Goni government and ultimately Evo Morales' election were also present, still united by their grief.

And then there were the two large gangs of unsavoury looking characters, noisily occupying one third of the green in cheap leather jackets and slicked back hair. They were La Paz's top criminals and narco-trafficking fraternities, here to honour their fallen. Death in their trade is an occupational hazard. The police eyed them nervously from a nearby roof top. The authorities could have cleaned up the city's mean streets in one fell swoop but on this day, more than any other, they were untouchable.

As soon as I met Maria and her skull I knew that I was in way out of my depth. A long time university lecturer, fierce feminist and defender of the Andean world, Maria sat imperiously on a small mound of earth. Her legs were crossed beneath her, giving the impression of a rather spindly Buddha. A gaggle of students were respectfully gathered around her feet, eager to soak up her every word.

Maria invited me into the group with a handful of coca, explaining that chewing coca is as much an act communication as consumption. Like the peace pipe in Native American communities, coca is used to mediate conflict in the Andes. 'You can talk of terrible conflicts for hours and hours until you reach a point at which you believe the issue is resolved,' she said. 'When you start to speak with coca you can't have double morals... you cannot lie with coca' she told us. 'If you do she will punish you.'

Maria indicated the skull at her feet that she was tending to with her students. Only this was no ordinary cranium. It was in fact far older than the cemetery itself, a pre-Columbian Aymara woman who had been recovered from a sacred burial ground. She looked, with her jutting lower jaw and badly chipped eye sockets, to be fairly cheesed off about being removed from her original resting place.

Maria admitted that she shared my unease. She found the skull twenty-five years earlier in an ancient *chupa* and took it home. It wasn't long before she fell ill. 'I went to a medicine man who told me that I had offended my ancestors by taking her out of the tomb without permission and had to either make a blood sacrifice with a llama, or baptise and adopt her as my ancestor,' Maria told me.

She went for adoption and the remains of the skull have been an important addition to the family ever since. 'Every Monday, Tuesday and Friday I light candles and ask her for good health and good luck with my work. If I am very busy and forget to look after her, bad things start happening to me,' she said.

Maria had been careful to make sure that her skull had been afforded every comfort. She had gently nestled it in a cradle of rose petals. Her attendants placed lit candles and scattered coca leaves all around her. 'Don't leave her out,' I was warned when I light up a cigarette. 'She's very sharp, doesn't miss a thing.'

I was encouraged to place two burning straights between her remaining teeth, together with two lit candles in front. We watched attentively until satisfied that they had been 'well smoked.' This was a signal that she accepted my presence amongst the group. 'We continue this cycle for eight days and then we say goodbye' she explained. 'This way the dead will be tranquil until next year.'

Maria was on a roll. 'The West has colonised us into thinking that only the man is masculine. They have colonised us into thinking that there is only one God. In the Andean religious world everything is sacred,' she said between long drags on her own cigarette. 'The world is sacred, the hills are sacred, the water is sacred, the dead are sacred, our ancestors are sacred,' she added. 'Together with our ancestors we are recovering our own sacred vision of the cosmos.'

I took my place on the ground near to her skull. The air was charged. It felt like these mourners were having a picnic at an open air festival, a far cry from cemeteries back home, spaces of neglect as much as they are of remembrance. 'You probably think that all this is grotesque,' Maria said with a wry smile. 'But what is more grotesque? Bringing the dead back into our lives, or gradually growing accustomed to their absence'?

I wasn't sure, but with a flight to London the next morning the moment had come to leave this extraordinary, high blown country behind. I wondered if this would be my last time here, or if I would one day return with my family to travel with my young son, Tom, to Bolivia. I sensed that like Monarch butterflies on their long migration up the western seaboard of the Americas, this journey across the Altiplano was taking several lifetimes.

The light was fading, the two candles guttering, their flames touching wick's end. There was just enough time to blow them out. To say one final goodbye, with a silent prayer, to my imperfect, most wonderful father. Perhaps, all along, this was the journey that I had travelled so far to complete.

EPILOGUE

My father grew up on Knockie Estate near Foyers, on the southern bank of Loch Ness. The 700 acre estate is made up of rough hill ground, mixed native woods and several small lochs full of brown trout and the odd pike. Although owned by the Grants of Glenmoriston ever since they bought it from the Frasers in1823, it was my great grandfather, Frank, who first decided to settle there in the 1920s.

Frank, who was brought up in Moy near Foyers, started renting Knockie from his older brother, Murray, in 1900 for long family holidays from his home in Cheshire. Just getting there back in the early 20th century was a big part of the experience. With no road on the south side of Loch Ness they had to take the steamer from the railway head at Inverness to the pier at Invermoriston. From there a signal would be sent to a boathouse on the other side of the loch and a boatman would row (aided by a small sail) across to pick them up. A pony and cart would them take them up a steep track, following a burn to Loch nan Laan high above Loch Ness. Beyond is the lodge, in those days a modest two-story house that dated back to around 1745.

Frank moved lock, stock and barrel together with his wife, Caroline, and their ten children into Knockie in 1921. Once there he threw all his resources into developing the farming side of the estate, creating more arable and pasture from the land to support sheep and cattle, including a new a dairy herd of little black Kerry cows. Frank also added a new West front to the house with twin 'pepper pot' bay windows and more bedrooms upstairs to make room for his Edwardian scaled family.

My grandfather Patrick (Pat) was the eldest of their five sons. Commissioned, aged eighteen, into the Royal Artillery at the outbreak of the First World War, he went on to spend much of his life fighting in foreign fields. Little is known of his experiences of the First World War, although being in the artillery meant he would have been spared the horror of the trenches. He went on to serve in the Middle East and India, only returning to the UK for a posting on Salisbury Plain in 1930.

Pat met his wife, Betty, at a tennis party near Salisbury and they were married in 1933. They were then posted to Newcastle on Tyne were my uncle Simon was born in 1935, my aunt Bridget (Biddy) in 1938 and my father Nigel in 1942. Dad must barely have set eyes on his dad who was away fighting with his regiment in North Africa for the six long years of conflict.

A war baby, one of dad's earliest memories was of planes thundering in the skies overhead. His sister Biddy was old enough to remember the confusion and uncertainty as they were moved around the country to avoid the bombing. At Crawley, near Winchester, she remembers being taken down into the cellar by her grandfather and listening to the distant thump of gunfire and bombs along the coast where there were attacks on Southampton and Portsmouth. It became too dangerous for her to go to her school in Winchester and the school was evacuated to Blair Castle in Perthshire.

When Pat finally left the army at the end of the war he decided to move to Knockie with Betty in the spring of 1946. Their Highland retreat must have felt like a haven of solace from the trauma and loss of fighting through his second world war. Pat lost two of his brothers while they were serving in North Africa. Jim (nicknamed Mouse), a captain in the 9th Lancers, was killed in his tank in the Tunisian desert. Frank, attached to the RAF, died shortly after being taken prisoner at Tobruk. And then in their first summer at Knockie came the devastating news that another brother, Hugh, had also been killed on duty in Kenya, stabbed with a spear while trying to settle a dispute between two Masai warriors over a cow.

A refuge for displaced aunts and cousins during the war, 'the big hoose' at Knockie was still occupied by Frank and Caroline when Grandfather Pat settled there with his family. Frank was still very active and although crippled by arthritis Caroline very much ruled the roost with an iron hand, often driving herself around in an improvised electric three-wheeled buggy.

Pat, Betty and the children were given the cottage alongside the Lodge, a cosy two up and two down with a temperamental open range in the kitchen and a small sitting room with an open fire. Dad remembered the wireless being turned on for the night's entertainment. His mother Betty would bring through a tray laden with mugs of steaming Ovaltine and a plate of biscuits to have by the fire before bed.

Despite the hardship of the post war years with a shortage of both manpower and basic supplies my father's early years were happy ones. His family were almost self sufficient, relying on the produce from the vegetable garden and meat from the farm. Biddy still remembers the little dairy with its wonderful daily routine of producing milk for the house and cottages, cream for making butter and cheese and skimmed milk for feeding calves. She loved taking dad in to watch the milk being poured through the 'separating machine' – a tower of revolving silver cones that dispensed skimmed milk and cream from different spouts. She described it as 'making the strangest of musical grinding noises, almost like an orchestra tuning up.'

The farm buildings with all their associated industry must have been fascinating to a young boy. In a letter to her grandchildren cousin Caroline Kilbrandon remembered:

"A forge and a carpenter's workshop full of shavings and glue. There was a saw-mill with a long bench and a wicked looking toothed circular saw. It could rip a huge larch log into wide sweet-smelling planks and it cut huge piles of birch wood logs for fires in the house. In another shed there were big stacks of peat, chocolate brown and shaped like bricks to burn in the fires in the winter."

Growing up in such a remote spot Dad, endearingly nicknamed Pudge, was always outside, often armed with a stick rod and jar of worms, or a basket to collect gull eggs from the island. In the summers he ran wild with young visiting cousins, ranging around Knockie like wolves in small packs. They would go fishing for brown trout in the 'roaring caverns' of the Ardochy burn, sail a timber built dingy on Loch Knockie or play high spirited games of kick the can across the stepping stones down the steep slope to the shore of Loch Ness. Dad would often scramble up *Beinnn-a-Bhacaidh,* the hill that looms opposite the lodge. Below a Munro in height *Beinnn-a-Bhacaidh* doesn't attract many hill walkers but there are rewarding vistas from the top of the hill of the length of Loch Ness lying far below.

For Dad the scramble up the ben's steep north face was his first encounter with that wondrous sense of isolation that haunts wild places. He told me that on one winter walk on the hill his collie took off after a stag. The stag quickly tired of ploughing through deep snow and the collie cornered it in a peat bog. Dad ran after trying to call his dog back, but by the time he reached the scene it was too late. The stag had killed his pet with single blow from one of its hooves and trotted off.

During the winter months the cousins vanished and Dad, Biddy and older brother Simon (when he was around) became inseparable. The highlight in the snow was the Christmas adventure to the holly tree on *Beinnn-a-Bhacaidh.* Biddy wrote that:

'The three of us, Simon, Nigel and I would set of with a large sack and a hook and saw, round the end of the loch and up the steep side of the hill to where a small clump of Holly bushes clung to the rocks. As this was the only form of decoration Mum would countenance we made the most of it and came home with a bulging sack of prickly branches. We always had a Christmas dinner and Dad would crack open a bottle of Grandfather's good claret. Sometimes, just once or twice as we grew up, I remember him tell a story of his wartime experiences.'

Biddy remembers one rare occasion when Loch Knockie froze over just enough to support their weight. She excitedly raided the attic bedroom with Nigel for discarded skating boots that would fit them and armed with a couple of kitchen chairs set off down the road to the loch side. Biddy wrote that 'nothing compares to the wonder of flying over the black frozen surface of the loch, over the white bubbles suspended in the ice and the weird boom set off by the pressure of our weight.' She told me that they edged up further towards the clear dark water in the centre of the loch until the ice's eeiry protests drove them back. Heading home she could still picture the 'last rosy light on the snowy hills and a cold streak of greenish blue to the north.' She went on to become a painter with the most delicate appreciation of colour.

Knockie was sold in the late 1960s, too much of a financial burden for the family to keep on. But those childhood years lived on vividly in my father's imagination. He once told me that at night he would lie in bed and imagine walking down the long corridors of the big house. He said that he could still remember the subtly different give of each door as he opened and closed them behind him.

My mother Lucy used to say that Nigel's childhood was too perfect. It left him with one foot in this distant hinterland and nothing in his adult life could quite match up to it. The more any of us tried to get close to him, the further he would retreat back into his world of hills, science and silence.

We turned west off the A9 a few miles short of Inverness, on the B851 to Foyers. Impossibly squeezed in the back of the tiny red hire car, I wondered just how my brother Charlie and his wife Jules had ended up in the comfortable seats up front. While they sat in front of me in pristine serenity I was squeezed between my two year old niece Coco in her oversized car seat on one side and my twelve year old son Tom, all bones and sharp angles, on the other.

As we drove into Stratherrick I was struck by how grand and expansive this country is on a spring day. It was one of those blue-sky afternoons in the Scottish Highlands when time seems suspended in a bright looking glass. The hills were lush and green after a long winter that had left snow bones clinging on with long fingers in the sheltered corries. The granite escarpments, flecked with white quartz, speckled the rounded bens like the fine camouflage on a songbird's egg in the sunshine. To top it all 'Arrival Theme' by Capercaillie struck up on the radio. It felt so good to be travelling back to my dad's old stamping ground.

When Knockie was sold shortly before I was born my Great Aunt Elizabeth kept hold of a small cottage, called Brackashie, on the shore of Loch Knockie as a holiday home for her extended family to visit. The cottage felt more like a bothy than a habitable home with a cramped kitchen, bedroom and bathroom upstairs. Down a short flight of stairs there was a narrow passageway leading to a single bed in a tiny room at the end. The bathwater was almost black with peat and the hall permanently smelt of rising damp, musty fishing tackle and wood smoke from the brick lined fire in the kitchen that never properly drew.

Thanks to Brackashie I was lucky enough to grow up exploring some of the same childhood haunts around Knockie as my father before me. During our stays at the cottage we rarely bathed (there wasn't enough hot water) and lived on oatcakes and tinned soup on a flip out orange Formica table by the kitchen window. I slept on the cramped camp bed in the downstairs corridor, crowded in by nets, cane rods, maps and odd wellies. I would ease myself under the damp covers at night with a justifiable sense of trepidation. There was no way of knowing what spiders or daddy longlegs had found their way in there for comfort.

There is a little stone pier nestled in birch woods at the bottom of the slope below the cottage. From here we would voyage in a green rowing boat around the loch on fishing trips, cap gun fights and explorations of the loch shores. I caught my first wild brownie on the loch aged six. Bigger expeditions made it all the way down to Big Beach and Heron Island in the lochs easterly reaches. I remember swimming off Big Beach and emerging with a huge (in my mind) leech hanging off one of my legs. I'm told I ran around so fast screaming in circles that nobody could catch me for ages to get the beastie off of me.

Dad was usually the instigator of these adventures, no doubt re-living his own youth at the same time. We would camp on the tiny circular island, thought to be a crannog, across from the cottage. He took us on long foraging missions for chanterelles alongside the Roaring Caverns at Ardochy. There were also countless yomps up *Beinnn-a-Bhacaidh* as we got a little older.

My favourite view of *Beinnn-a-Bhacaidh* is from a boat on Loch Knockie. I remember pushing off from the pier with Dad at night to get a clear view of the fine filament of stars that were dusted above the hill's ragged outline. A faint Milky Way gleamed in the loch's oily black surface. Phosphorescent tracers chased after my hand as I drew it through the dark water. My father was just a shadow, pulling deep on the oars.

Once we paid a visit to the Fraser yew tree, marked on old maps as the 'oldest yew in the north.' It is located somewhere along the shore of Loch Ness in amongst thick native woodland. Finding it requires a knowledge so intimate of the local topography that I doubt I could now find my way back to it without one of the original Knockie Grants, like Dad or cousin Annabel, leading the way.

I had expected a single huge tree but the Fraser Yew has long since divided into a multiple of trunks under a single canopy. A particular silence held that space that only an ancient yew grove can express. Dad showed us the heart tree with a knotted hole in the centre. Inside was stored an old whisky bottle filled with poems, prayers and love notes. This is said to have been an old trysting spot between the Frasers and the Invermoriston Grants in the distant past. There was also a half-finished bottle of Highland Park with a couple of glasses. We shared a dram, topped up with a splash of water from the nearby burn.

When I got into my late teens and Dad's visits to the UK were only on fleeting business trips I would go to Knockie under my own steam with friends. Once we caught a train to Inverness and only managed to hitch as far as Dores by the evening. We ended up walking though half the night to reach the cottage. My uncle Simon was often in residence at Brackashie on these visits and made a fantastic host. Much more outgoing than my own father he would regale us with tales of family exploits in between bouts of frenetic drumming on his *bodhran* to his favourite ceilidh bands, played through a tinny cassette player in the kitchen.

These late-night sessions were always accompanied by a bottle of Famous Grouse. I still remember his top tip to getting through life was to 'always keep a bottle of the creature under the sink.' Simon died a few years before my dad of a heart attack, aged only 58. But in my mind his spirit still strides the bright tops of *Beinnn-a-Bhacaidh* with his *bodhran* and a plentiful supply of 'the creature' strapped to his back.

There isn't much to the village of Whitebridge apart from the Whitebridge Hotel, a classic Victorian pile with a long veranda by the entrance. Inside the walls are adorned with bucolic landscapes, stuffed fish and an impressive array of antlers around the main hall light. The cosy wood-pannelled bar is the main draw to tourists and locals alike, where solid Scottish fare is cheerfully washed down with the local Happie Chappie ale. The dimly lit pool room next door has been the scene of many a legendary contest between Grant cousins over the years.

But we weren't there for the beer and pool. We had come to rent the hotel's boat, a forlorn looking grey rowing boat that lay waiting for us on a bed of mud and pond weed in the scrappy birch woods that fringe Loch Knockie. It has been resting there in my mind's eye for some time, a somewhat modest craft for our long planned ancestral journey.

It is hardly a long or arduous feat to row across the narrow loch to my great-grandmother Caroline Grant's secret garden on the far side. It would have been far simpler to just walk around the shore. But there is something about the emotional draw of the loch's black waters that tugged at my heart, together with the last lines of a poem that I had read years before at my father's funeral service.

Dad had specified in his will that he wanted his remains to be returned back to his beloved Knockie. So a year after he was cremated in Chile we respected his wishes and buried his ashes at Drumtemple burial ground near Foyers. The cemetery is on a hill, next to a small stone kirk, the Dores and Boleskine Church of Scotland. A high stone wall encloses the graveyard with two mature trees arched above the entrance. Follow the gravel path to the wall on the far side and there is a small collection of headstones dedicated to the Knockie Grants. It is a beautiful spot, looking south east across *Loch Mhor* with commanding views of the hills beyond. Little has changed from this outlook for generations, until the *Stronlairg* windfarm arrived to spin lazy white circles across the horizon.

Dad's headstone with the dedication of our clan motto 'Stand Fast' lies flat on the ground next to his brother Simon. The stones directly behind are dedicated to both their parents Pat and Betty and grand-parents Frank and Caroline. Dad's marker is weathering well, although it was laid slightly uneven and one corner has been eroded back by successive encounters with the church lawnmower.

I don't remember much about Dad's remembrance service in the gloomy kirk. At one point I stood up and read *The Watersong Ends* by Dad's favourite Chilean poet, Pablo Neruda. We emerged afterwards, blinking into the shifting Highland light to a lone piper playing Lord Lovat's Lament by the stone dyke. I felt adrift, deafened by the crunch of my own boots across the gravel. It was only a few yards but each step yawned a thousand miles wide. In the end it was Neruda's last stanza that carried me to the graveside.

"It is time, love, to break off that sombre rose,
Shut up the stars and bury the ash in the earth;

*And, in the rising of the light, wake with those
who awoke
Or go on in the dream, reaching the other shore
of the sea which has no other shore."*

Luckily the hotel's boat was stable enough for us all and Charlie and I pushed off with Jules, Coco and Tom perched happily on the back. We used the heavy wooden oars to punt the boat past the shallows and clear of the reeds. The wind picked up and ruffled the water as we moved further out into the bay. Charlie shifted forward to sit next to me and took up an oar, joking that between us we made up 2GHP (Grant Horse Power).

Leaning back into each stroke we set the boat to the wind and our intention to reach the secret garden on the far side. My great grandmother Caroline had two grand ambitions in her life: to have a big family and to create a beautiful garden. She realised both dreams, not only raising ten children but also finding time to design and nurture a stunning garden from the thin highland soil.

She chose around four acres of uneven land on the northern side of the loch, not far from the Lodge. The boundary was built with high stone walls and a fence on the western side to keep out the sheep and deer. Her garden evolved gradually over twenty years into a magnificent space with a criss-cross of golden yew trees at its centre and a network of paths edged with long herbaceous borders.

Hugely knowledgeable about plants, Caroline's garden attracted visitors from all over the country through the National Garden Scheme in the early 1950s. My aunt Biddy still remembers the garden in its heyday. She ran around its grassy paths as a child, helping to weed the borders and day-dreaming on the old swing under the cherry tree. Without her memories there wouldn't be anything left to uncover apart from some broken down walls and a decaying wooden summer house.

The stone pier in the far bay had all but tumbled into the water but we still managed to disembark awkwardly and pull the boat out of the water. We struggled through the thick undergrowth of young rowan, bramble and bracken that had crept down to the shore. With little Coco's help we found a small metal gate with a broken latch, half buried under a Rhododendron. The actual fence had long disappeared but this little wrought iron gate felt like a portal through a worm-hole into our collective past.

We clambered beneath a big fallen birch and a chestnut tree, both Tom and Coco excitedly picking up miniature baby frogs in the grass along the way. Ever attentive to the needs of her family Caroline transformed these lower stretches of the enclosure into an extensive kitchen garden, providing an abundant supply of fresh vegetables to the community at Knockie.

Glass houses, cold frames and raised beds were put in to aid food production through the short growing season. In the summer the garden produced plentiful kale, root vegetables and soft fruits. Dad and Biddy were sent down to pick raspberries for jam in the autumn and to dig tatties out of the frozen earth in the winter.

We eventually found an entrance of sorts to the main garden with steps and a broken-down wall, beyond evergreen trees, old and gnarled, crowded in around a clearing. The scraggly avenue of yew trees remained and the cherry tree that once supported the swing for visiting children still forlornly offered up its fruit. It was hard to imagine this garden in any former glory when it obviously hadn't seen a set of pruning shears in 60 odd years.

Back in its day the transition from the kitchen to ornamental garden was marked with exotic fir trees, including an enormous redwood and a monkey puzzle that still stands today. A terrace was built in with steps running up to the flower garden. Here Caroline set beds into gravel paths with rare alpines as well as bright profusion of primula, gentians and blue sapphire. Biddy especially remembers the pink, white and mauve phlox, interspersed with tall stands of white thistle.

At the heart of Caroline's now secret garden we found the remains of the wooden summerhouse with the roof falling down around the old range. It remains a well-proportioned space with big windows that would have been a welcome escape from the rain and midges. Biddy remembers Frank escaping here from the constant demands of the farm to read Virgil, a cuckoo clock on the wall marking the passing of time. He would leave the space smelling sweetly of pipe smoke and cedar.

But the summer house was Caroline's domain. Peering through the cobwebbed window it was easy to imagine her taking a break from tending to the beds with her worn hands. By today's standards she would dress formally for gardening in a white blouse with a cardigan and a tweed skirt. She always wore a fob watch on a tight chain around her neck.

Very much the matriarch of Knockie, Caroline must have cast a formidable presence with her sandy hair pinned back and striking blue eyes. Despite being confined to a chair by arthritis in her later years Catherine's authority never dimmed. Biddy remembers her sitting by the range, propped up with pillows and with a blanket over her knees. Although affectionate towards her grandchildren they were always a little scared of her.

The garden's decline was inevitable once Caroline's health and indefatigable energy started to falter. For a while her brilliant gardener, Sam Mackintosh, picked up the slack but when he retired the family struggled to keep up with the weeds. The kitchen garden was the first to go and then over time the paths grassed over and the wild wood crept back in. Frank passed away in 1952 and Caroline followed him four years later.

I caught up with Charlie, Jules and the children at the bottom of the avenue of yew trees, in a square enclosure made up of low stone walls. The space was framed by big corner stones with granite spheres perched on each of them. In the centre was a three metre tall concrete column, topped by a sun dial on each of its four faces. It was overcast and many numbers below the dial's brass pointers were obscured by lichen. But on a sunny day it still casts a shadow as crisp as when it was first erected back in 1948 to mark Caroline and Frank's golden wedding anniversary.

The sundial at the heart of the secret garden is said to have been designed by the architect Sir Basil Urwin Spence, slightly better known for reconstructing Coventry Cathedral after the war. Although a very modest structure to claim this sort of lineage, the dial does have ingenious little bird baths built into the top of the wide base. The plinth is an octagon with a set of initials ornately carved into each of the sides. They look at first glance like masonic symbols, or the individual sums of a far more complex mathematical equation.

Tom and Coco were already on their hands and knees, brushing away the tall grass to reveal the lettering.

I took out a pad and noted them down, guessing that they were family initials. It took a conversation with Biddy when I got home to properly decipher them. They are the initials of Caroline and Frank, together with all of their sons and daughters with their respective husbands and wives. One of the sections combines their two sons who were killed in the war and died single, Frank and Jim (Mouse) Grant.

Pat and Betty, my grandparents are listed and I can place a few of the other names, like Edward who survived the Second World War only to turn to the bottle and commit suicide in the heavily haunted Boleskine House in the 1950s. I remember great aunt Cat at an advanced age living on the island of Seil. I also met great aunt Elizabeth who built a second cottage next to Brackashie and lived there well into her 90s. But what became of the other names and their descendants are a mystery to me. Dad was one of as many as 42 first cousins descended from Caroline and Frank's long and fruitful marriage.

To me the sundial in Caroline's secret garden is this long-dispersed family's heart stone. I much prefer this more ambivalent structure, still angled skywards to catch the sun, to a cold slab of finality in a church yard. The runes around its base trace the intricate web of lives that have travelled out from this secluded corner of the Scottish Highlands. Dad's trajectory from Caroline's sundial in the secret garden is only one of these stories. His grandchildren Coco and Tom's narratives continue now to spin on beyond him.

A gust of wind picked up in the trees and rolled through the leaves around us like the whispering of ancestors. I imagined Caroline, the matriarch who wished for a big family and was blessed with ten sons and daughters, standing here and looking on beyond her long years. The evening light is in her eyes. She reflects on her children and their descendants' many journeys, like fine threads of silver gossamer taking flight from the white thistles in her beloved garden. I wonder if she senses that, one way or another, all of us would eventually return home.

Born in the Star Mountains of Papua New Guinea and raised in Devon, Scotland and the United States, travel has always been in Jamie's blood. After studying for an MA in Latin American Studies he worked as a journalist in La Paz for three years where he wrote for the Economist Intelligence Unit. Previous books include *Winter in Glen Lyon (2014)* and *Summer in South Georgia (2016)*. Jamie won the Marie Hedderwick Travel Writing Award for an extract from *Altiplano* in 2016. He lives in the Scottish Highlands with his wife and son.